Bladens in Ireland

by Karen Proudler

First Published in Great Britain in 2015
by Karen & Graham Proudler
Forge Cottage, Field Farm, Aston Lane, Shardlow
Derbys   DE72 2GX
Copyright © Karen & Graham Proudler, 2015
ISBN: 978-0-9566831-7-5

CONTENTS

Introduction

1. South Derbyshire   1

2. Newton Solney..............................   7

3. Ireland   19

4. New England.............................   25

5. The Irish Rebellion.......................   29

6. Mayor of Dublin   51

7. Dr Thomas Bladen   65

8. Difficulties   67

9. Loftus-Bladen Marriage   73

10. Other Bladens   83

    Epilogue   87

    Appendices   89

    Chronologies   93

Acknowledgements

To the Bodleian Library, The Board of Trinity College, Dublin, House of Lords Parliamentary Archives and Helena Coney for collaborating in our joint Bladen and Bladon interests in South Derbyshire. Also thanks to the various local record office staff for being so helpful.

Abbreviations

Abp	Archbishop
Bp	Bishop
CARD	Calendar of Ancient Records of Dublin
CSP	Calendar of State Papers
DLS	Derby Local Studies Library
DRO	Derbyshire Record Office
HMC	Historical Manuscripts Commission
IMC	Irish Manuscripts Commission
LRO	Lichfield Record Office
NLI	National Library of Ireland, Dublin
PRO	Public Record Office (TNA)
SRO	Staffordshire Record Office
TCD	Trinity College Dublin
TNA	The National Archives
UML	University of Manchester Library

Note:

The names Bladon and Bladen are both used throughout this book as they appear in original sources; though generally those family members in Ireland adopted the Bladen spelling, whilst most relations and ancestors favoured Bladon.

INTRODUCTION

The Bladens arrived in Dublin in the mid-1620s and quickly established themselves, and their business, amongst the mainly English Protestant settlers based in the city. For many years they were the sole book-sellers and held the monopoly on official printing. Head of the family, William Bladen also held public office as an Alderman and later Mayor and, from his business premises in Castle Street, was well placed to seek sanctuary for his family inside Dublin Castle walls when Rebellion broke out in 1641.

This book is a collection of notes and records of those early settlers and describes their origins and what led the Bladens to leave their ancestral home in central England. It also contains transcripts of letters, written by William to his son who was in England overseeing the family's print business in London, describing what life was like for the family in Dublin. William and his eldest son Thomas were both trapped, in separate places, during sieges in January 1642 and William's accounts of what they endured was quite harrowing. His son had the letters published and distributed in London and those stories played a part in shaping the history of the times in the Civil War years.

**Bladon Field area in Winshill
near Burton-on-Trent**

Reproduced with permission of Staffordshire Record Office
D(W)1734/2/3/139, Anglesey Collection, maps made by William
Wyatt between 1757 and 1760

1. SOUTH DERBYSHIRE

The Bladens' journey to Ireland began in the small agricultural village of Newton Solney on the south/east bank of the River Trent where it is joined by the smaller River Dove just a short distance away from the brewing town of Burton-on-Trent in England. Situated next to a ford which traversed the converging rivers, Newton Solney[1] and its environs are at the very edge of the county of Derbyshire where it meets Staffordshire, though early Bladens in this area paid scant attention to county boundaries in their movements.

**Site of an ancient ford across the Rivers Trent/Dove
at Newton Solney**

---

[1] The name Newton Solney was originally derived from the Old English word 'Niwantune' meaning New Farm. Then from 1300 onwards the Solney was added by the holders of the Manor, the de Solneys (Soleni, Sulene, Solny or Sulney variations in spelling). Newton Solney Conservation Area Character Statement 2011, South Derbyshire District Council

Following the river's winding path from Burton in Staffordshire and Winshill[1] (the southern part of which was administratively moved from Derbyshire to Staffordshire in 1894) along to Newton Solney and further east to Repton in South Derbyshire, the Bladens (whose relations mostly adopted the Bladon spelling) had been settled along the bank of the River Trent since the earliest times.

Indications are that the surnames Bladon and Bladen sprang from a specific location between Newton Solney and Burton-on-Trent in an area within Winshill called 'Bladon' or 'Bladonfield'. This place-name was established by 1250 (probably earlier) when it was mentioned in a land grant between William de Winsul and Robert de Rolleston, and there is further mention of it in a land grant dated 1291 where both Newton Solney and Bladon were granted to Alfred de Solney by the Priory at Repton.[2] The name probably derived from the topography of the area in that Bladonfield is a hillside running towards Burton and, in Latin, 'Bladon' translates as the 'side of a hill.'

Although the larger area which envelopes Bladon, called Winshill, existed as a village from at least the 11th century,[3] there appears to be no surviving evidence of Bladon itself having once been a distinct or well populated settlement. It seems rather to have been a descriptive name for a collection of fields which are spread out on the hillside. Today it consists of just a few farms or later structures which have adopted the Bladon name: for instance, Bladon Farm, Bladon Castle and Bladon Cottages which have taken their name from Bladonfield. All of these buildings were constructed long after those with the Bladon surname had moved away, but they are evidence that the family once dominated the area.

Early documents mention 'Blaudon Field' (1250),[4] 'Blandon' (1301), 'Blawdon' (1438) and Blaudonfield (1400s).[5]

---

[1] Domesday Book entry: Derbyshire, 324, i, 273r (3-3) Burton Abbey: Winshill (Staffs) TRE and TRW the Abbot of Burton has a Manor in Winshill which is assessed at two carucates. King William put (*apposuit*/set) six sokemen [tenants holding land in feudal tenure] there, who belong to Repton

[2] Private Every family papers, cited in 'Newton Solney' by Michael Day and Maxwell Craven, 2009 as ref PEC XLIX

[3] See above Domesday Book entry

[4] Staffordshire Commissioners referring to Domesday Survey entry. Also referred to in a land grant from William de Winsul to Robert de Rolveston as Blaudon Field

[5] DRO: D5236/11/7/1-2, 15th Century schedules of land in Newton Solney

Kenneth Cameron in 'The Place-Names of Derbyshire' was unable to track the precise etymology of the Bladon name beyond citing 14th century occurrences and suggested descriptive adjectives of *"cold, cheerless hill, v Bläw, dun, though the development is not clear"*[1] again derived from the translation from Latin. One constant, however, throughout the centuries has been the field names which include: Far Bladon Hill, Bladon Close, Lower Bladon Close, Upper Bladon Close, Bladon Sitch, Near Bladon Fields etc[2] (see map in Introduction) and, through a variety of Indentures, court rolls and chancery documents, it is clear that numerous members of the Bladon family owned or had an interest in land in this area right up to the 1600/1700s, after which time they mostly drifted away to surrounding villages and towns.

What strengthens the likelihood of this being the place where the Bladon and Bladen surnames originate is the combination of a distinct area called 'Bladon' with a group of ancient field names bearing the name and, equally, the presence of families with the surname being in the same place as far back as written records began.

Whilst it is difficult to place individuals accurately on a family tree with any certainty from the 1300s, the ancestral trail of those Bladens who went to Ireland can be worked back to a certain extent, at least to the early 1500s in Newton Solney. Although individuals taking their name from a particular place may not have originally been from the same blood-line of descent, in the case of Bladons there does appear to be a long linear line of descent (along with the equally ancient local family of Boylston) present in this small agricultural community, as can be seen on the chart on page 4. There is also evidence of the evolution of the name.

The history of these two particular families was bound together for many centuries, not just by marriage, as they were also in each other's Wills and Indentures and, as early as 1500, they were sharing a tenancy of the principal messuage and surrounding farmland in Newton Solney.

---

and fieldnames

[1] The Place-Names of Derbyshire, Part 3, Kenneth Cameron, Cambridge University Press, 1959

[2] DRO: D(W)1734/2/3/139 by William Wyatt between 1757 and 1760, shown in the Introduction

Boylstons and Bladons in Newton Solney

Thomas Boylston fl.1360-1390 = Margery Land grant from John Lathbury 1390s			Richard Bladon fl 1353		
John Boylston c1390 Egginton Manor Court Roll of 1401			Thomas de Blaudonlone (or Thomas de Blawdon) fl 1385-1404. Probably the same Thomas from records in 1353 (D5236/4/24)		
William Boylston c1416-76 + John Bladon signed Sir Nicholas Longford's NS land claim DRO: D5236/4/42			Adam Blawedon (de Blawedon) fl1438-41[1] Attorney to John Lathbury	John Bladon c1416-76 with William Boylston at Sir Nicholas Longford's court 1476	
Thomas Boylston Snr 1430-1500+ = Margery Original lease 1466 for 3 lives combined with Mathew Bladon's lease 1500, land grant in NS from John Lathbury DRO: D5236/4/41 1475, present at Manorial Court UML: CRU 547 DRO: D5236/4/45 land rented by Mathew Bladon and Thomas Boylston to pass from Lathbury to Longford 1500			Richard Bladon 1475 - present at Manorial Court with Thomas Boylston UML:CRU 547	Matthew Bladon Joint tenant with Thomas Boylston re capital messuage NS	John Bladon fl 1505 (elder) sued by Ralph Longford for cutting down wood, 'late' of NS, so maybe moved to Winshill[2]
Thomas Boylston Jnr c1470=Alice Shephard=James Burton, Lyndley 1508 house lease for 89 years from Repton Priory DRO: D5236/4/47			John Bladon (younger) 1558 - Mentioned by both Richard & Henry Boylston in Milward v Boylston		
Thomas Boylston	Richard Boylston c1506->1566 =1540= Joan Pipe. Named as a life on parents' house lease. Milward v Boylston deft in 1558	Henry Boylston c1515->1566 mar'd Marjorie Bladen in 1566. Milward v Boylston deft in 1558	Richard Bladon d1566 made Richard Boylston (left) his executor		
	John Boylston 1580: renewed grandfather's lease (of 1508)	Henry Boylston d.1592. Will witnessed by Thomas Bladen, Hen. Byard yngr, Edw. Goodrich	Thomas Bladen (nephew of above) Witnessed Henry Boylston's Will 1592		

---

[1] Common Pleas, Easter, 18, Henry VI, PRO: CP 40/717 m.391 dated 1440. Adam Blawedon appeared by his attorney against a debtor

[2] Common Pleas, Hilary, 20, Henry VII, PRO: CP 40/971 Ralph Longford v John Bladon and others (Richard Beynard, late of Newton Sulney, William Ilkesley, late of Newton Sulney), 1505 'in a plea whereby by force of arms they broke into a close of the said Ralph at Neweton Sulney'

There follows an exploration of some of those early records which demonstrates the evolution of the name. The picture is not a complete one but, in presenting these notes on early records, it is hoped to show why the indications that Bladons originated in this place seems so strong.

It took some time for Bladon as a surname to evolve and settle and the earliest instances of the surname were diverse, ranging from Balenone, to Blawdonlone to Blawdon. There was some inconsistency in records with the same individual appearing in one record as Bladon, such as in court rolls from the early 1300s, then elsewhere being called Blawdonlone.[1] One early mention in 1438 was of Adam, who was an Attorney to John Lathbury (Lord of the Manor, as were the Longfords).[2] No doubt an ancestor of the Bladens who went to Ireland, and probably many other Bladon branches too, it is clear that Adam's surname was derived from the place-name[3] when he was described as 'Adam de Blawdon de Newton Solney'.

Good evidence of the evolution of the surname has been found in a 16th Century chancery document where members of the Boylston family were challenged over ownership of a piece of land. In Milward v Boylston,[4] dated 1557-79, brothers Henry and Richard Boylston, who had inherited land called Haxley at Newton Solney made reference, in their deposition of ownership of the land going back some four generations, to a time when it was owned by a Bladon. This is of interest because they claimed the property passed from the ownership of Repton Priory to 'John Balenone alias Bladon'.[5]

---

[1] UML: CRU 543, 544, 547, 234 John Rylands Library, accessed by H Coney

[2] DRO: D5236/9/21 Lathbury appoints Adam de Blawdon as his Attorney

[3] Lichfield Joint Record Office: B/A/1/12 f.233v, f236r, f238r and f240r, Register of Bishop John Hales of Coventry and Lichfield, Lichfield Cathedral, Orders to celebrate Ember Day, John Bladon. Bladon's name appears on 22nd December 1487, 1st March 1488, 31st May 1488 and 20th September 1488 as an officer of the church on the four Ember Days. These were days of fasting and abstinence set aside each year to give thanks to God. Francis Mershman, 'Ember Days' The Catholic Encyclopaedia, Vol. 5, New York: Robert Appleton Company, 1909

[4] TNA: C3/129/69 Milward v Boylston

[5] References to Balenone as an early version of the surname Bladon calls to mind early names appearing in Branston (south of Burton) where the 1532 'A List of Families in the Archdeaconry of Stafford 1532-3' edited by Ann J Kettle, lists a family with the name Balenden

This description of Bladon as 'alias Balenone' conveniently links the variation in name with earlier mentions of, for instance, Blaudenlone through the preceding four hundred years.

The above statements in depositions are given added authority when it is considered that one of the men giving evidence, Henry Boylston, was himself married into the Bladon family[1] and whose wife may have been a direct descendant of the John Bladon referred to. Whilst there were instances of individuals being recorded as Bladon in the 1400s, the names were in still in flux. In 1385 there was a 'Thomas de Blaudonlone[2] de Newton Solney' (of Bladon lane), also referred to as Thomas 'de Blawdon'.

The Bladons and the families they intermarried with, not surprisingly, dominated the area of Bladon-in-Winshill. As an isolated agricultural community with a small population in the mid-1550s of only 84,[3] at least 14 had the Bladon name whilst most of the remaining residents were related in some way. That number eclipsed those Bladons still remaining in neighbouring Newton Solney at the time. At least that is how it appears from records, as many of the Bladons in Winshill had their events (baptisms, marriage and burials) recorded at Burton-on-Trent whilst others nearer the top of Bladonfield and Winshill were nearer to Newton Solney and consequently had their events recorded at Egginton Church (the main church across the ford) or even at Repton towards the east. It was to be many years before Newton Solney emerged as an autonomous district for record-keeping purposes.

---

[1] Margaret Bladon and Henry Boylston married 4th February 1566 at Egginton

[2] SRO: D(W)1721/3/30/13 Feoffment

[3] SRO: B/A/27ii. A List of Families in the Archdeaconry of Stafford 1532-3 edited by Ann J Kettle, MA., Lecturer in Mediaeval History, University of St Andrews; 1544 Rental of Possessions of Burton College showing tenants in Winshill D(W)1734/3/3/28; SRO D(W)1734/2/3/21B Easter Book for Winshill etc and D(W)1734/3/3/3 covering the periods 1532, 1544 and 1560

2. NEWTON SOLNEY

The Bladens who went to Ireland were part of the community spanning the small area from Winshill to Newton Solney, most of whom were yeoman farmers. Whilst undoubtedly being descendants of those mentioned in the Bladon/Boylston chart on page 4, the following is as far back as the line can be worked with some certainty:-

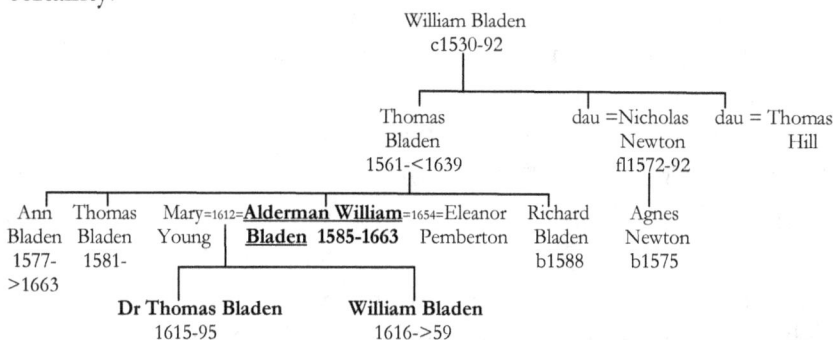

```
                        William Bladen
                           c1530-92
                               |
        ┌──────────────────────┼─────────────────────────────┐
     Thomas                 dau =Nicholas      dau = Thomas
     Bladen                     Newton              Hill
    1561-<1639                 fl1572-92
        |                          |
 ┌────┬──────┬─────────────┬──────────┬──────────┐
 Ann  Thomas Mary=1612=Alderman William=1654=Eleanor  Richard   Agnes
Bladen Bladen Young     Bladen 1585-1663  Pemberton   Bladen    Newton
1577-  1581-      |                                    b1588     b1575
>1663             |
          ┌───────────────┬──────────────────┐
      Dr Thomas Bladen        William Bladen
         1615-95                1616->59
```

William Bladen (marked above in bold and underlined) made the journey to Dublin and it is possible to glean some insight into how his ancestors lived before this from records of his grandfather William, who died when William was just 7 years of age. William (the elder) was present at many of the manorial courts held by the Longford family. Indeed on 2nd May 1564 Nicholas Longford held a 'Great Court of Newton Sulney'[1] and, present along with Longford was Richard Needham of Snitterton and his wife Dorothy.[2]

---

[1] DRO: D5236/12/19 Court roll for Great Court at Newton Solney

[2] DRO: D5236/4/56 lease from Richard Needham of Snitterton, gent, and Dorothy his wife to Thomas Leigh (her son) of Egginton for the term of Dorothy's life for a fee of £20. Dorothy was a Longford cousin, being a Lathbury descendant, and had been married firstly to William Leigh of Egginton and it would be from her descendants that the Egginton Manor would pass later to the Every family

In attendance to pay homage was William Bladen (along with Richard Bladen,[1] a brother or cousin), both of their names appearing frequently together in documents of the time.[2] A few years later in October of 1577 both William and Richard were again present at another court when a formal agreement was thrashed out.[3] The tone of the agreement gives the impression that the Longfords ruled their Manor with an iron fist, as every single issue raised came with the threat of a fine for non-compliance. As expected in a rural farming community, issues mainly concerned management of cattle, the common ground and water courses. The Lord of the Manor, however, took the opportunity to impose deadlines for his tenants to observe good husbandry. Those attending to pay 'homage' to the Lord agreed that no-one should fish in the Trent without permission of the farm owners along the river bank nor take away their catch and that no person or persons should cut down any wood in Bladon [Wood], on pain of paying a forfeit. It was also agreed that *"evrye yarde in the medow be fensed"*, *"that the wheat fields be fensed before Saynt Luke's Day next"*, *"that the pease fields be fensed before the Feast of Saynt George"* and that *"evrye man secure his water course before the Feast of Martinmas next"*. Not all Bladons, however, observed the rules and some were involved in disputes over cattle rights, cutting down trees and taking wood from Ralph Longford's[4] woodland preserve at Bladon.

William Bladen (the grandfather) was a prosperous yeoman farmer and sufficiently well off enough to employ two servants. His age at death, though not known for certain, can be estimated to be perhaps 60 or more as he made bequests to his *"children's children"* in his Will which is reproduced at page 91.

---

[1] In 1577 Richard Bladen had been involved in the manorial court and presided over fines issued to various fellow farmers for transgressions. One of those issued with a fine was Nicholas Newton (shown on the chart on page 7) who was fined over a leasing issue at May Day. UML: John Ryland Library, CRU 553

[2] DLS: Deeds 3423 Newton Solney, Set 5, No. 43, 2 May 6 Elizabeth (1564) p39. In full at DRO: D5236/12/19 Court Roll for Great Court at Newton Solney held for Nicholas Longford Esq, Richard Needham, gent, and Dorothy his wife. Dated 2 May 6 Eliz I [1564]

[3] UML, John Ryland Library, CRU 553, 13 Newton Solney Tenants' Agreement

[4] Sir Ralph being the father of Nicholas Longford mentioned

It is possible to approximate the family's residence from references in his Will to the Pynfold and Dale Bridges (which he left small sums of money to improve) and which seems to be in that area at the bottom of Bladon Field where it runs into Winshill. Present-day Bladon Farm, built long after 1592 when William wrote his Will, is located within 200 metres of that area. The pinfold at Winshill in 1598, just a few years later, stood at Winshill Green which is just yards away.[1] Also south of the present-day Bladon Farm[2] and Bladon Farm Cottages there is Dale Brook (which was later used to demark the Derby/Staffs boundary when Winshill was split within the two counties in 1894) and north-east of Bladon Farm is Dale Farm,[3] so the Will pin-points the area at the very heart of Bladon Field where this family had a messuage. The area is criss-crossed with small brooks and a ditch watercourse which channels the rainwater running down the hill and William's donations for bridges would be to facilitate access across those waterways which, at times of high water levels in the River Trent, were prone to flooding, exacerbated by surface water run-off from Bladon Hill.

A proposal to build 100 houses[4] in this specific area was rejected in 2015, no doubt for a variety of reasons, but flooding assessments taken in the course of report preparations indicated the site was classed as being in Zone 1 of the Environment Agency's Flood Map and consequently considered more vulnerable to flooding. A group of local residents campaigned to reject the proposal and they were successful. If the development had proceeded it would have covered the entire area from Bladon Farm to Dale Brook, some 6.5 hectares.

---

[1] SRO: D(W)1734/2/3/112d, f29v (cited in www.british-history.ac.uk/vch/staffs/vol9/p204)

[2] Bladon Farm: J. W. Shepherd & Son, Bladon Farm, Wheatley Lane, Burton-on-Trent DE15 0RS

[3] The Dale name (originally recorded as Dole), like Bladon, may have given rise to local families who adopted the Dale name. Fraser refers to Dale (Short and Long Dale) being in existence from 1216-72 and a 13th century deed referred to these closes as being situated near a brook. Field-Names in South Derbyshire by William Fraser A.R.Hist.S. 1947

[4] Barratt Homes North Midlands. Proposed Residential Development, Newton Road, Winshill, Burton-upon-Trent. Flood Risk Assessment prepared by EWE Associates Ltd., Final Rev A, October 2014

It seems highly likely, therefore, that this Bladen family were resident at or near the location of today's Bladon Farm. Although the messuage they occupied no longer exists it would have needed to be large enough to accommodate a family with two servants and be sufficiently close to Dale Brook for William to be concerned about access in the area.[1] Next to the present-day farm is the location of the open field or common land where tenant farmers would have had grazing rights. The three common fields in the area would have been part of the farming practice of the medieval period of the three-field system of crop rotation: Bladon being one, Dale and Hough being thought to be the others.[2] In the case of Bladon Field, the open land amounted to some 50 acres.[3]

Returning to William Bladen's Will, he made mention of his daughter who had married Nicholas Newton, another equally ancient family whose name was probably taken from the village.[4] One of the witnesses to the Will was Robert Bladon of Winshill. Robert died a few years later without leaving a Will but there was an appraisal taken of his property on 20th October 1591 by Robert Bakewell[5] (who leased the substantial Bladon family holdings on Bladon Hill which is about to be discussed)[6] which showed him engaged in husbandry producing crops, no doubt for the benefit of the Burton brewing industry at the bottom of Bladon Hill.[7] In 1588 Robert Bladon was one of three men from Newton Solney and Winshill who were called to muster for the Spanish Invasion and the Armada expedition that took place in August of that year.

---

[1] The only other potential existing property in the immediate vicinity is 'The Old Dairy'/Bladon Paddocks, which fronts Newton Road or The Old Stables (between the Dairy and the Farm House)

[2] Field-Names in South Derbyshire by William Fraser A.R.Hist.S. 1947. Fraser records it as The Howgh but notes Every Deeds of 1821 recording as Hough (one of the three Common Fields)

[3] www.british-history.ac.uk/vch/staffs/Vol.9/pp202-204

[4] DRO: D5236/4/57 Indenture between Nicholas Newton and Thomas Leigh for messuage in Newton Solney, dated 1572 for 21 years. The messuage comprised of one cottage, two crofts and a rood of meadowland for the payment of 16 shillings yearly

[5] The following may be a reference to the same family's long-standing presence in the area: DRO: D3155/6099; Fine ref Robert 'Blackwell' and wife Mary for 32 acres of land and 4 acres of meadow in areas including Bladon, 24th June 1495

[6] DRO: D5423/1 &2

[7] LRO: Inventory for Robert Bladon of Winshill, date 1592

He was listed as 'calliu'. The other two were Thomas Eaton (Corp.) and Richard Sharpe[1] (Ar.), both from families that the Bladons married into.[2]

There may be more to William's story in the sense that records exist of a William Bladen of Newton Solney and William Jackson of Stapenhill having Writs of Habeas Corpus served on them in 1582[3] over a cattle dispute. Disputes over cattle, and where they were allowed to graze, were common enough in agricultural communities where the village common could become overcrowded, but in 1581 the records show that a serious problem had developed involving William Bladen and others.[4] The matter concerned Thomas Duport and Thomas Hamp on one side and William Bladen, Thomas Dutton, William Jackson and John Mogge on the other (Mogge family held land in Newton Solney which passed from the Bladons to the Boylstons, previously mentioned in Milward v Boylston). The Hamp and Bladen names appear next to each other on Paget rental lists[5] for Winshill as neighbours and the families had been very close. In William Hamp of Winshill's Will of 1556 (father of Thomas), Robert Bladen had been one of the parties who took Hamp's Inventory of goods after his death and Robert Fitchett (Bladen relation and Hamp refers to him as 'my neighbour') had signed as a witness to Hamp's Will.[6] Thomas Duport was a lawyer whose family family had estates in Shepshed and Queniborough in Leicestershire and he was a man of great influence, having been the executor of Lady Mary Grey's Will.[7]

---

[1] SRO: D(W)1734/2/2/8-9 Burton Manor and Mickleover Paget Possessions. William Sharpe's widow Alice married Richard Bladon of Winshill in 1547. Another Sharpe (Margaret) married William Bladon of Winshill also in 1547

[2] Journal of the Derbyshire Archaeological and Natural History Society. 1896, Vols 17-19, Muster for the Spanish Invasion 1588

[3] SRO: D603/L22 Writ of Habeas Corpus to take William Jackson of Stapenhill and William Bladon of Newton Solney, 2nd May 1582

[4] TNA: STAC 5/D34/33 Duport v Dutton, Mogg and Bladen, date 1581

[5] TNA: E178/3103 County Survey, Paget Possessions, Winshill

[6] Will of William Hamp, 1556, Winshill, Litchfield/Staffs Record Office

[7] Thomas Duport 1513-92 of Shepshed and Queniborough, Leics. Servant of Henry Grey, Marquess of Dorset and later Duke of Suffolk. He was also Receiver of the Duke of Suffolk's western lands (1553), he was also servant of Henry, Lord Berkeley and Commissioner IPM Leicester in 1571. He was a kinsman of the Grey family and practiced law in Leicestershire, being heavily involved in land transactions. MP for Truro 1554. The House of Commons 1509-1553, Vol. 1,

The problem between the parties centred on an area of ground that had been used by Dutton, Jackson, Bladen and Mogg for grazing their cattle. The matter had been brought before the Justices of the Assize in Derby around 1580 and, during the course of proceedings, it was later claimed that Thomas Dutton (of Winshill),[1] William Jackson (of Stapenhill), William Bladen (of Newton Solney) and John Mogg had committed perjury and in this respect Thomas Duport (with the backing and support of Thomas Hamp) brought a Bill of Complaint into Chancery against the above-mentioned men.[2]

As part of the legal wrangling that ensued, writs of Habeas Corpus were issued:-[3]

WRIT OF HABEAS CORPUS - Royal Writ of Habeas Corpus to take William Jackson of Stapenhill and William Bladen of Newton Solney, 2nd May 1582.

Both men were detained in Derby Jail whilst the matter was further investigated. In response to a second legal challenge over the issue, all the defendants (Dutton, Jackson, Mogg and Bladen) all vigorously denied having committed perjury at the Derby Assizes, rather suggesting that if there had been perjury it was between Thomas Duport and Thomas Hamp (stated in all the depositions). There is also reference to Robert Bladen in the above papers, though the context is not clear and he is not cited as a defendant. The only Robert Bladen at that time would have been in Winshill and the disputed land may have been in that area.

---

p69, edited by S.T. Bindoff

[1] TNA: PROB 11/187/165, Will of Thomas Dutton of Winshill, Proved 30th September 1641, written 9th April 1640 'Memorandum of Thomas Dutton: The day and yeare above written, Thomas Dutton of Winshill in the County of Darbie, being weake but of good and perfect memorie being desired to make his Will he sayd his Will was soon made for he desired that his wife should pay his debts and, after his debts payd, he sayd he would give the one half of his goods remaining to his wife, and the other half to be equally divided among his children; and being asked whether his wife should bring them upp out of her half or not he left it to her discretion and being asked what he would give to the poor he sayd a noble or an angel whatever they pleased on the like in effect and purpose, the year first above written. Thomas Fitchet his mark, Susannah Heal witnessed

[2] TNA: STAC 5/D38/9, D38/36 and D34/33, dated 1581

[3] SRO: D603/L22 Habeas Corpus writ for William Jackson & William Bladen

Pitchfork Hugh

The above case saw Hamp and Bladon on opposing sides and there are records of the Hampe family being in Winshill from at least 1556[1] and several Hamp and Bladen families resided in close proximity to each other over the decades.[2] There was even a marriage between Margaret Hamp and Hugh Bladen at St Modwen's Church in Burton-on-Trent, but perhaps the Duport dispute soured relations because a few years after the above incident, in 1591, another member of the Hamp family brought another Bill of Complaint against some more of the Winshill Bladons.[3] William Hamp alleged that Hugh Bladon, son of Robert and Joan, assaulted a man over the tenancy of a property. The man was attacked with weapons and so severely wounded that he died from his injuries some weeks later, never regaining the power to divulge who his attacker was. Among those named with Hugh Bladon was Elizabeth Fitchett, Robert Fitchett and John Bladon.

Although there was more than one individual in Winshill called Hugh Bladon (at least two or three and all closely related), another similar incident occurred very shortly after which strongly suggests the same Hugh Bladon was involved. Robert Abbott brought a complaint against Hugh, his wife Anne, mother Joan Bladon and Hugh's sister (in-law) Margaret Bayley alleging that on a recent visit to Winshill, the Bladons ambushed him in the streets of Winshill and, together with another eight or so individuals, assaulted and beat Abbot causing him great injuries. It was claimed that the three Bladon women restrained Abbot whilst Hugh prodded the poor man with a pitchfork resulting in Abbot losing his right eye and leaving him with one inch of the tool's grain lodged in his head.[4] Hugh and the others denied all charges against them.

As to what may have prompted Hugh and his relations to attack Abbot (if indeed they did) there are a couple of possibilities. It is believed that Robert Abbott's wife was Agnes Gilbert and not only were there Gilbert neighbours in the small hamlet of Winshill, but

---

[1] LRO: B/C/11/Wm. Hampe (1556)

[2] TNA: E178/3103 dated 1583-5 County Survey, Paget Possessions, Winshill and TNA: E164/41 Survey of Paget Manor Lands

[3] TNA: STAC 5/H1/38 Hamp v Bladon. William Hamp v Hugh Bladon, dated 1591-92

[4] TNA: STAC 8/44/8 Abbott v Bladon, dated 1599/1600

there was also a marriage between a Hugh Bladon and Isabella Gilbert. The County Survey of Paget Possessions in Winshill[1] shows a John Gilbert residing in the area and there could well have been a connection between all these Gilberts and it may have been a neighbour dispute.

Another possibility, which has yet to be discounted, concerns an incident that happened many years earlier in Devon. A Bladon family had taken occupation of a messuage on the manor of Stoke St Nectan:-

Property at Hartland leased for three lives:
1) George Bladon, 2) Anne Bladon and 3) Johan Bladon.

The property was part of the lands of the monastery at Hartland which had been granted to William Abbott. Following the upheaval of the dissolution of the monasteries by Henry VIII, the King had granted the lands to Abbott who had been the King's Sergeant of the Seller.[2] The Bladons, upon the death of John Keyn the previous occupier, took their residence after his death. This was probably 1549 (being the second year of the reign of Edward VI mentioned in documents). The Bill of Cause raised subsequently by the Bladons describes a group of 30 men, led by William Abbott and relations Patrick and Thomas Snow, gathering at the Bladons' house with 'staves, swords and other weapons' and forcibly 'took out the said Anne Bladdon and also the wyffe of the said George Bladdon beying there'.

The Bladons were ejected from the property and not allowed to recover any of their possessions, their goods and chattels being retained by William Abbott. Although that particular William Abbott died without heirs, his property and title passed to his wider family and, if the above mentioned Robert Abbott (injured at Winshill) was connected to those at Hartland, then the Bladon relations of Winshill may have had a powerful motive for revenge.

---

[1] SRO: E178/3103 dated 1583-5 Paget Possessions in Winshill
[2] TNA: STAC 3/7/19, dated 28th January 1547 to 6th July 1553

14

Thomas Bladen (yeoman) d1639

Son of the above-mentioned William and father of Alderman William, Thomas left no Will[1] but in many of the Bladon Wills at this time mention was made of the 'ghostly father' or 'gostley farder'. In the case of John Bladon the elder (probably a cousin of the subjects of this book) for example, this was a reference to a Prior called John Davenport. When John's son came to write his Will some years later John Bladon the younger made a bequest to Prior Signor Raufe Clerke. The small agricultural community of Newton Solney only had a Chapel of Ease called St Mary's (from 1271) which came under the auspices of the Repton Priory so the Priors would have ministered at the chapel but would also have been responsible for dispensing advice and spiritual support. The description of the Priors as 'Ghostly Fathers' was common practice at the time, as can be seen in Shakespeare's 'Romeo and Juliet' where Friar Lawrence mentions his 'Ghostly Father'.

When John's brother Richard Bladen wrote his Will in 1566 the same Raufe Clerk signed his Will as a witness and again he was referred to as 'my gostly father'. Ralph Clerk was a pensioned former Canon and number two at Repton Priory[2] until the time when Henry VIII began dissolving the monasteries. At the crucial moment, in 1538, the head of the Priory John Young (1508-38)[3] died just three days before dissolution. Young had been attempting to prevent the Priory's destruction and a large fine (£266-13s-4d) had been paid to the King to assuage him. These moves were successful to a limited extent as certain manors, messuages and advowsons were alienated by license. However, having received the money and made some concession, the King resumed his plan to dissolve the Priory after all.

---

[1] There is a 1639 Admon to Alice, widow of Thomas Bladon of Newton Solney. If this is the same Thomas, then he probably married twice, his first wife being the mother of his children (including William) and Alice being his second wife. Alice re-married after Thomas Bladon's death to Henry Byard. Both Thomas Bladon and Henry Byard appear on the 1592 Entitled Assessment of the Hundreds. Harpur Crewe Papers and also TNA: E179/93/293

[2] Clerk is listed on www.theclergydatabase.org.uk as follows: Radolph Clerk, Repton, 1558 stipendary (LRO, B/V/1/2 Liber Cleri)

[3] The Heads of Religious Houses, England and Wales, Vol. III: 1377-1540, p512. Ed. David M Smith (Cambridge: Cambridge U.P. 2008)

Young's death at such a juncture must have seemed like an unhappy omen and Clerk could hardly have assumed the job at a worse moment and so it was by his hand that the papers were signed to end the Priory's almost 400 years of existence.[1] The fact that the Bladens had the sub-prior of Repton, albeit the man who was forced to oversee its dissolution, involved in their Wills may be indicative of their (or some in the family)'s high status in the community.

Before leaving the subject of Bladens and Bladons being in Newton Solney, as the story of the Bladens in Ireland moves away from the area, there is one last development to mention regarding the family's apparent decline in the area. In Michael Day and Maxwell Craven's 2009 book 'Newton Solney' it was stated that the Bladon family *"fades from sight after at least four hundred years in the parish."* Indeed, as has been shown, they were present from the 1300s to 1600s in Newton Solney but by the 1500s they had a larger presence in Winshill. Even there, however, the family's name was declining as individuals with the surname moved away. One document in particular seems to mark a watershed when numerous Bladons relinquished their interest in the area. In 1599 an Indenture of Lease and Release conveyed property away from Bladons to the Fitchett family who were close relations and the following shows the extent of the land holdings Bladons relinquished at this time (see map of area in the Introduction):

Half an acre	Oxen Croft with the hedgerow on the side and all the hedge by estimation lying in Winshill
6 lands at	Weadley, with hedge lying in common field called Mill Field
3 lands	Mickle Marsh Flat - with hedge adjoining and lying in said Mill Field
1 rood land	Mill Way Flat, lying inside Mill Field
¼ rood	Box hedge lying in Mill Field
4 lands	Bladon Close, hedgerow lying in Bladon Field in Winshill
1 land	Bothom Land, lying in Bladon Field
3 pikes land	Dale Yeld, lying in Bladon Field
1 land	Dimple Flatt, with hedge lying in Bladon Field
1 land	Yokmyres Croft head and hedge lying in Bladon Field
1 land	lying at the Ditch, hedge and ditch lying in Bladon Field
1 land	Bladon Sitch, lying in said Bladon Field *(location of present-day*

---

1 Established in the 12th century, the surrender of Repton Priory by Ralph Clerke, subpr. and can. took place on 25th October 1538. TNA: E322/200, L & P Henry VIII, XIII(2), p260, no. 688, DKR 8, app. ii. p38

Bladon Farm, Wheatley Lane, Winshill)

2 lands	New Dole in Bladon Field
1 land	Red Hill, with hedge lying in common field called Crakehole
1 land	Peas Hill, lying in Crakehole Field
1 land	lying upon the Oak with hedges in Crakehole Field
4 lands	lying at the Ditch in Crakehole Field
4 pikes land	Paddocks, hedge running onto land called Paddocks
2 roods	Meadow ground lying in Winshill Meadow
1 bovate	In pasture called Quarries and Ashley[1] on Trent side, Winshill

As can be seem from the above, just one branch of the Bladon family held ownership of a large swath of Bladon Field and the interesting aspect of this document is that it was co-signed by some 16 individuals (in addition to other witnesses), most having the Bladon name or who were relations by marriage. The implication here being that those parties had some interest in the conveyance as, of those signatures which can be read, all have some familial connection to the Bladon family.

There followed a second document (release) dated 7th April 1600 whereby the estate was conveyed to William Fitchett. Interestingly this document includes reference to a messuage which again reinforces the presence of at least one large, extended Bladon family connected with Bladon Field. There were hardly any farmhouses in the area in 1600 with Bend Oak Farm, The Grange and Winshill Great Farm being later structures situated on the other side of Bearwood Road in the direction of Burton.

---

[1] SRO: D4533/1/5/1-2 Feoffment by John Rotheram to William Bladon and William Goodriche dated 27th October 1599 for £200. SRO: D5434/1 and 2 Bladon and Goodriche to Fitchett, date 1600. Indenture from William Bladon c1520->99, his son-in-law William Goodryche (who had married William Bladon's daughter Agnes b.1533) in 1576 BoT p.r. The two Williams covenanted with John Rotheram (one of the Six Clerks of Her Majesty's Court of Chancery; recorded as Rotheram throughout the documents but he signs himself as Rotherham) to convey Bladon land for £200 to Fitchett. Robert Bakewell had been the previous tenant, so tenancy may have reverted to Crown or Lord of the Manor. Rotheram was either the owner of some land at Winshill or, perhaps more likely, acting as agent for the Lordship's Manor. He was not merely an attorney facilitating the conveyance as the feoffment refers to Rotheram ordaining to "constitute ordain appoint in the stead and presence my trusty and well beloved in Christ our Walter Kynerton Clerk and Thomas Richard, yeoman, my true and lawful attorney and attornies, jointly and severally for me". Signatories to the Feoffment included Edward Bladon whose name frequently occurs with that of William Goodriche and was possibly a brother of Agnes Goodriche (née Bladon)

An examination of the Indenture dated later (the Release) shows a plethora of Bladon relations putting their signatures to the second document, including: Roger Houlte, Richard Atkin,* William Eaton, John Bladon younger, Richard Bladen, Edward Bladen, Francis Bladen, Thomas Warde (elder),* Thomas Warde (younger),* James Fitchett, John Henshaw, William Haws, William Henshaw, William Bondwaste and Robert Fitchett. *Neighbours of the Bladons in Winshill.[1] This list of names is in addition to those four individuals called on to witness the deed and is likely to be some kind of family settlement. Indeed 12 of those named above are related to Bladens and it is only the others whose names cannot be read too well that presently have an unknown connection.

Although the above conveyance to the Fitchetts represented a large slice of Bladon holdings in Winshill and Bladon Field in particular, it was not all. Division of property and land meant that other family members retained acres of land in the area, such as Francis Bladon for example who, though residing in Repton in later years, retained ownership of Newton Solney land.[2] It does, however, seem to show the majority of family members relinquishing their interests and, for the most part, severing the family's long association with the specific area of Bladon Field.

This was the family then that Alderman William Bladen was born into and he will be discussed next.

---

[1] TNA: E178/3103 and TNA: E164/41 Surveys of Paget lands and possessions
[2] DRO: D5236/18/7/2, dated 13th April 1719. Indenture Henry Byard, Francis Bladon and Elizabeth Fisher

3. IRELAND

William Bladen 1585-1663

Our subject of interest, William Bladen, was not the first Bladen to make Ireland his home as records from 1379 show a William Bladon present in Dublin. That particular Bladon, whose origins are unknown, was a Chief Magistrate/Bailiff there during the reign of King Edward II.[1]

From the Bladen family of Newton Solney, two younger sons of Thomas Bladen, yeoman, were sent off to London as apprentices to the print/stationery trade.[2] 'Our' William and his younger brother Richard were both baptised in Egginton church, across the river, though the family resided at Newton Solney.[3]

The Register of the Company of Stationers states *"William Bladen, son of Thomas Bladen of Newton Solney in the county of Derby (yeoman) hath put himself as apprentice to Arthur Johnson citizen and stationer of London for eight years from the Feast of Phillip and Jacob Apostles Last"* (1 May 1602).[4] Arthur Johnson had himself only been freed from the Stationers Company the year before and so may only have been eight years or so older than his new apprentice.

---

[1] Working alongside him was John Wydon who was the Dublin Provost and by 1380 Wydon had become Mayor. The History and Antiquities of the City of Dublin: From the Earliest Accounts Compiled from Authentick Memoirs, Offices of Record, Manuscript Collections and other unexceptionable Vouchers by the late Walter Harris Esq, 1766, p499

[2] A Dictionary of Members of the Dublin Book Trade, 1550-1800; based on the Records of the Guild of St Luke the Evangelist, Dublin, Mary Pollard, 2000

[3] Stationers Company Records (in 1602) refer to William Bladen being the son of Thomas Bladen (yeoman) of "Newton Solney" rather than Egginton. Many Bladen and Bladon events from Newton Solney residents were recorded at the main church across the ford in Egginton

[4] Arthur Johnson left William £1 in his Last Will and Testament (9 Feb 1631, proved Prerogative Court in Dublin)

William and his brother Richard may have had relations already residing in London as another Bladen was recorded as being in the same business in London already. Robert Bladen, son of John was an apprentice in 1594 and appears in London as a resident there and who completed his apprenticeship on 23rd July 1606. His training began some six years before William and ten years before the other Newton Solney brother Richard. Date-wise it is possible that this is the Robert Bladen who appeared in Yorkshire a few years later and began a line of descent there.[1]

At some point during his apprenticeship William was transferred to John Symons, bookbinder,[2] though this was perhaps a secondment to learn additional skills, as Bladen retained his contacts with Arthur Johnson long after his apprenticeship was completed.[3] Brother Richard was apprenticed to a nearby printer called Humphrey Hooper in 1604.[4] William completed his training and was freed from his apprenticeship by 7th May 1610[5] and shortly afterwards he married Mary Young on 13th April 1612 at St Bride's Church, Fleet Street, London[6] which was just a few minutes away from St Paul's Churchyard, the centre of London's book-trade, where William was

---

[1] Robert Bladon or Bladen born about 1579 at Ludgate, London, father John c1550-1617. Records of the Court of the Stationers Company

[2] Derby Local Studies, Card Index

[3] A Dictionary of Members of the Dublin Book Trade, 1550-1800; based on the Records of the Guild of St Luke the Evangelist, Dublin, Mary Pollard, 2000; also Apprentices and Freemen of the Company of Stationers of London 1562-1640

[4] Apprentices & Freemen of the Company of Stationers of London 1562-1640

[5] A Dictionary of Members of the Dublin Book Trade, 1550-1800; based on the Records of the Guild of St Luke the Evangelist, Dublin, Mary Pollard, 2000. Another record states he obtained his freedom on 16th April 1610

[6] Marriage record states: William Blaydin and Marye Yonge married 13th April 1612 at St Bride's Church, Fleet Street, London. Young Family: There are frequent mentions of various members of a Young family though it is difficult to say for definite if these relate to William's first wife Mary. In Eleanor Bladen's Will of 1667 (William's second wife) she refers to a Richard Young of Dublin, Solicitor. CSP records transactions with Dr Thomas Bladen (William's eldest son) and a Richard Young age 65 in 1653, therefore born 1588. There is also a description of Richard's brother John (who died in Barbados) as having no issue and being his only brother and heir. In addition, 3 Jan 1653/54 further bond by John Young (draper) for £200 to the Protector Cromwell (Irish Adventurers). Stationers Company records show his in-laws as William and Mrs Young. Richard Young assigned his share of the Barony of Armagh to Thomas Bladen of Rainham in Kent. CSP ref Adventurers 1642-59

based. Stationers Company records show that his new in-laws, William and Mrs Young, stood surety for William's loans from the Guild (right through to the period 1626-31).[1] Guild loans were at a very attractive low rate of interest and the Young family probably had some connections at the Stationers Company as a Roger Young was auditor of accounts there.

William quickly established himself as a printer and stationer, the roles being combined in those days, and from 1612 he was in partnership with John Royston in the book trade.[2] His shop was located where all the other London booksellers were at St Paul's Cathedral Churchyard where he traded by the great north door at the sign of the Bible from 1612-24.[3] This was the old St Paul's Cathedral which was to be destroyed in the Great Fire of London in 1666, not the present-day structure. The churchyard was once a favoured place for burning to death martyrs to their faith[4] and was a popular meeting meeting place and central hub of the book-selling industry which, as well as catering for the domestic market, sold to North America, the Caribbean, India, Africa, Australia and the Far East markets.

In addition to the bookshop, William rented a house for £15 in Bay H, which was called the Latin Shop[5] and he was located close to Arthur Johnson's shop[6] which was similarly described as being "neere "neere to the great north door of Paules at the sign of the white horse."[7] Also in close proximity was Jaggards (where a Robert Bladen was also in print apprenticeship), just a few yards away;[8] Jaggards[9] had printed, without permission, some of Shakespeare's

---

[1] Stationers Company Court Book C, pp 52, 187, 229 etc

[2] British Library record for Enchiridion Medicum - 1612

[3] H.R. Plomer's "A Dictionary of the Booksellers and Printers from 1641-1667"; COPAC article reference Francis Bacon, printed by William Bladen

[4] Record of the Court of the Stationers Company 1599

[5] Rents Bay H (The Latin Shop) with a William Barratt, each renting a house

[6] Compeers by Night Series - Part III. Francis Bacon and the Secret of the Ornamental Devices by Mathew Walker, August 2002

[7] Ibid

[8] Records of the Court of the Stationers Company 1599

[9] Jaggard, William c. 1568-1623. Printer and publisher to the City of London. Although it seems likely he had previously pirated some of Shakespeare's works, he was chosen by the editors of John Hemming and Henry Condell as publishers of the First Folio edition of Shakespeare's plays. He died before the work was completed. This book, undertaken after Jaggard became blind, preserved 18 of the plays and corrected many textual errors in the plays printed in the earlier editions

works.[1] The previously mentioned Robert Bladen was, in 1595, in apprenticeship to Jaggards (Jaggers) printers and, although no evidence of a link in these two Bladen lines has yet been found, it seems highly likely that there was a close connection.[2] There is a record of Robert embezzling from his employer in 1599.[3]

With the help of his Young in-laws, who acted as guarantors for loans to get his business started, William was now fully trained and freed to trade by the Stationers Company. One of the earliest books William printed was in 1614, when he was just 29 years of age, and the author was Francis Bacon. Samuel Pepys was also known to frequent the area at this time and his diary shows a brief meeting with "a" Mr Bladen of Ludgate Hill.

About this time William's eldest son Thomas was born and the young family spent their early married years living in the shadow of St Paul's until the early-mid 1620s. During these years, 1618-19, William paid several visits to Ireland, on behalf of the Stationers Company, before deciding to make the move with his family there.[4]

In August 1626 William was preparing to leave London to go to Dublin to join his former apprenticeship master Arthur Johnson who had set up in Dublin as Factor of the London Company of Stationers in 1624[5]. The decision to leave London at this time may have been encouraged by the fact that it was not a healthy place to reside. Plague deaths were rising and it is possible that William lost family members to it, so however many members of his family were left, they all went to Dublin with him.

There had only been five printers in Dublin prior to Bladen's arrival: Humphrey Powell, William Kearney, John Franckton, Felix Kingston and Arthur Johnson.

---

[1] Record of the Court of the Stationers Company 1599

[2] Boyd's Inhabitants of London; Apprentices and Freeman of the Company of Stationers of London 1562-1640

[3] Record of the Court of the Stationers Company 1599 *"It is ordered that Mr Stokes shall pay to Mr Jaggard in recompense of all form offence and losses done to Mr Jaggard by Robert Bladen, his apprentice. Bladen, Robert, apprentice to J. Jaggard, to be taken back by his master on Stokes indemnifying him against embezzlement."*

[4] Irish Type design: A history of the printing types in the Irish Character by Dermot McGuinne, 1992

[5] Stationers Company Court Book C, p167

Franckton successfully applied for the patent to be King's Printer in Ireland in 1603 and one of his residences/properties was at Castle Street (where the Bladen family were later to trade from).

By 1618, however, the London Company of Stationers, of which Bladen was a member, was challenging Franckton's patent claiming *"wee are informed his Majestie's printer there is a person not fit for that office, both in respecte of his weake estate and of his insufficiency otherwise"*.[1] It was to be two years, just before Franckton's death, before he relinquished his patent to his deputy Felix Kingston. Kingston was only in post for a short time before Arthur Johnson arrived in Dublin and Bladen became Johnson's assistant,[2] or partner, and armed with a large stock of books, set out to establish himself as an agent for the consortium of London printers.

After Johnson's death in 1631 (he left Bladen £1 in his Will) and on payment of a £10 fine, William was freed of the City of Dublin on 22nd April 1631[3] and was obviously well settled and his business was thriving. By 1637, Bladen had been elected an Alderman of Dublin and for most of the years he traded in Ireland, William was the only book-seller and printer and he managed to keep trading through the turmoil of rebellion and the tumultuous change from Monarchy to Commonwealth, then back to Monarchy again.

To replenish his fast-selling stock, William imported books from Chester in 1634 and 1639[4] and three years later he was elected Sheriff.[5] On 2nd September 1639 William was admitted to the livery of the Stationers Company[6] and, shortly afterwards, bought out the other partners of the Irish stock agreeing to pay £2,600 for the stock, of which it was recorded he only paid £974-5s-8d by 1642.[7]

---

[1] Acts of the Privy Council 1618-19, pp64-66

[2] A Dictionary of Members of the Dublin Book Trade 1550-1800; based on the Records of the Guild of St Luke the Evangelist, Dublin, Mary Pollard 2000

[3] CARD and The Church of St Werburgh Dublin by Rev S.C. Hughes, 1889

[4] A Dictionary of Members of the Dublin Book Trade, 1550-1800; based on the Records of the Guild of St Luke the Evangelist, Dublin, Mary Pollard 2000

[5] A Dictionary of Members of the Dublin Book Trade - as above; CARD and the Church of St Werburgh, Dublin by Rev S.C. Hughes, 1889

[6] Court Book C, p327

[7] H.R. Plomer 'Some Notes on the Latin and Irish Stocks', Library 2nd Series 8, 1907, pp295-97

He thereby acquired the patent for being the King's Printer in Ireland, at least for official state publications if not for the business of general book printing.[1]

William's private and business address in 1643 was Castle Street which, as the name suggests, abutted Dublin Castle. Connecting to it was Werburgh Street (William's address in 1659)[2] and Fishamble Street which is where St John the Evangelist Church is located and was the burial place of his eldest surviving son Dr Thomas Bladen, and the wife and two children during the period 1677-1695. This location was also right next to City Hall which no doubt facilitated William's close involvement in local government.

So throughout the decades of this Bladen family's residence and trading in Dublin, they remained in a confined area in the heart of the city in close proximity to the safety of Dublin Castle.

---

[1] CARD, III, 391
[2] IMC Census of Ireland

4. NEW ENGLAND

When William took over from Johnson in the 1630s and became the King's Printer, everything was going well for him. He had been appointed Sheriff of Dublin, a post which would later be held by Thomas Pemberton in 1642;[1] this Thomas Pemberton was a relation (probably son) of Eleanor Pemberton who William Bladen would marry in 1654 as his second wife. Like Bladen in 1647, Thomas Pemberton would go on to have a stint as Mayor (jointly with Sankey Silliard) in 1649-50.

By this time Bladen was prosperous enough to employ servants and in 1637 he sent his servant James Redway[2] over to New England where he instructed him to buy land there and have a house built on Bladen's behalf. Redway[3] went to Hingham in Massachusetts, 13 miles from Boston[4] in 1637 but he did not travel alone, he went with Ralph Woodward. On 18 April 1637, an agreement was drawn up between William Bladen, John Fisher and Ralph Woodward,[5] all of the City of Dublin, Ireland that Bladen and Fisher would contribute

---

[1] The History and Antiquities of the City of Dublin: From the Earliest Accounts Compiled from Authentick Memoirs, Offices of Record, Manuscript Collections and other unexceptionable Vouchers by the late Walter Harris Esq, 1766, p506

[2] There was a system in place in Maryland (from 1630-1700) whereby "the person paying the passage and the servant signed a written contract, called an "indenture", both received a number of acres of land. The servant, however, would have to work for a period to pay back the person who had paid his passage. Thereby both parties had an inducement, both parties would be awarded acres of land. After a period of servitude (up to 5 years), the servant would gain his freedom - by this method both James Redway and Alderman William Bladen both gained acres of land from the Colonial Government. (www.dollarhide.com/family/histone.htm)

[3] James Redway 1616-84

[4] Article reference "James Redway of Dublin Ireland and Rehoboth, Massachusetts"; The Pioneers of Massachusetts; Suffolk Deeds

[5] Ralph Woodward born 1601 in Dublin, died 1661 in Hingham, Plymouth, Massachusetts. He went to Hingham in 1636 and later became a Dean. He sold his interests in Dublin in the late 1650s

money to Woodward so that he, his family and servants could go to New England. Once he was in New England, he was to "*provide proportions of land, in some other place, for himselfe and the said William Bladen and John Fisher ... and shall erect and build houses both for himselfe, and likewise for ye said William and John upon the said land ...*"[1] Both Redway and Woodward settled in Hingham.

Gaps in records make it impossible to know precisely what happened next but clearly some settlement connected with Bladen was established because two years later, in 1639, a man called Edmund Hubbard of Hingham gave his power of attorney to William Bladen to act on his behalf over his wife's son's Lyford inheritance.[2]

John Lyford 1590-1628 was born in Ireland and, though it is not known if he himself attended Trinity College Dublin, it is known that his son Obadiah (born 1617) was a scholar at Trinity in 1635 at the same time as William's son Thomas Bladen was there.

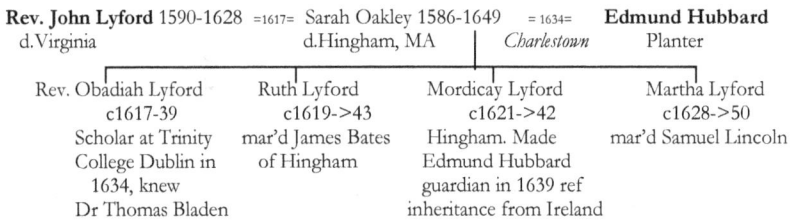

Rev. John Lyford 1590-1628	=1617=	Sarah Oakley 1586-1649	= 1634=	**Edmund Hubbard**
d.Virginia		d.Hingham, MA	*Charlestown*	Planter

Rev. Obadiah Lyford	Ruth Lyford	Mordicay Lyford	Martha Lyford
c1617-39	c1619->43	c1621->42	c1628->50
Scholar at Trinity	mar'd James Bates	Hingham. Made	mar'd Samuel Lincoln
College Dublin in	of Hingham	Edmund Hubbard	
1634, knew		guardian in 1639 ref	
Dr Thomas Bladen		inheritance from Ireland	

John Lyford married a woman called Sarah Oakley. John Lyford left Ireland to settle in Plymouth (Boston area near Hingham), then on to Nantasket, Salem and finally to Virginia where he died in 1628. Since Alderman William Bladen probably did not arrive in Ireland till 1626 it is doubtful he knew John Lyford personally, but their sons would have known each other; his son Obadiah attended Trinity with Dr Thomas Bladen. After John Lyford's death, his wife Sarah married Edmund Hubbard, a planter. Hubbard thereby became step-father to his wife's children Obadiah, Ruth, Mordicay and Martha. However, within five years of their marriage, Obadiah was dead. 18 year old Mordicay named Hubbard as his Guardian (or maybe Hubbard did

---

[1] All quotes are from Suffolk Deeds, Vol. III, pp176-7, from David R. Jansen's North East United States Genealogy for full article

[2] The Great Migration Begins: Immigrants to New England, 1620-33. Vol. 1 by Robert Charles Anderson. 1995

the naming).[1] Then in 1639, in order for Mordicay to secure a family inheritance from Ireland (Lyford family), Alderman William Bladen was given power of attorney to act on Mordicay's behalf. Edmund Hubbard described William as .... *"our well beloved and trusty friend William Bladen, alderman of the city of Dublin and John Fisher citizen of the same city to demand any inheritance due to Mordecay, particularly rents from lands in County Tyrone and the lease at Leballeglish in the County of Armagh so that the Hubbards need not be compelled to travel forth of the jurisdiction of the Massachusetts Bay in New England"*.[2] Note: John Fisher was William Bladen's partner in the 1637 venture to buy land in New England.[3] To entrust William with collecting an inheritance suggests a very strong connection/friendship, either between the eldest son Obadiah Lyford and Dr Thomas Bladen forged at Trinity or/and friendship between Mordicay's step-father Edmund Hubbard himself and Alderman William Bladen. The reason for mentioning the Bladen family's connection with the Hubbards will become clear in the following section 'Link lost to Bladens in America'.

Link lost to Bladens in America

Although it is known that those individuals tasked by Alderman William Bladen and his colleagues to go to New England did make the journey and settle there, it has so far not been possible to establish if any of William's descendants also went. The Hubbards did move on from Hingham to settle in Virginia and snippets of information show, for example, that some twenty years after the above mentioned Hubbard-Bladen dealings, there was a Joseph Blayton doing business with a Mr Hubbard in Virginia in 1663, but evidence to confirm this Blayton had any connection with the Bladens in Ireland has proved elusive.

---

[1] Taken from a Summary of genealogical matter in Lechford's notebook which identifies English homes of early settlers in America

[2] The Great Migration Begins: Immigrants to New England 1620-33, Vol. 1 by Robert Charles Anderson, 1995

[3] Article reference "James Redway of Dublin Ireland and Rehoboth, Massachusetts"

The combination of the large loss of Irish records and an equally large loss of records in the American Civil War have combined to stifle any progress at making connections. Currently there is a 120 year gap from Joseph Blayton[1] in 1663 in Virginia to the ancestors of the current Bladon lines.[2]

---

[1] Cavaliers and Pioneers; Abstracts of Virginia Land Patents and Grants 1623-1800 (Nugent 1934). John Horsington gent, 1750 acres, New Kent Co. 17 Apr 1663 Upon branches and main swamp of Black Creek beg. in the line of Thomas London by Westover Path running nigh an Indian field etc to Mr Hubbard's land etc., transportation of 35 persons; Joseph Blayton

[2] Further record: death of a William Blayden, New Haven Connecticut, this William was born about 1641. A Genealogicial Dictionary of the First Settlers in New England before 1692, Vol. 1, pp198-209

5. THE IRISH REBELLION

Whilst the men despatched to America to acquire land were making the journey and settling themselves in New England, William and his family faced problems at home.

Ireland was not immune from the political turmoil that was developing into a crisis in England in 1641, on the contrary it was part of it. From their prime location on Castle Street at the entrance and drawbridge to Dublin Castle, Bladens had as their neighbours, firstly Sir George Radcliffe from January 1633, followed soon afterwards by Thomas Wentworth (later Earl of Strafford) who was appointed Lord Lieutenant of Ireland in the 1630s.

Radcliffe was a close confidant of Wentworth and had been sent to Dublin in advance to prepare the ground for the Lord Lieutenant's arrival. Before leaving for Ireland, Radcliffe had been close to both Robert and Elizabeth Bladen of Yorkshire, being Elizabeth's cousin. It is thought that those Yorkshire Bladens, in the early years of their marriage, resided for some time with Radcliffe's family at Overthorpe Hall Thornhill as the families were very close.[1] There are numerous letters between George Radcliffe and his mother where the Bladens were mentioned, including references to their common ancestor Philip Waterhouse and his wife Helen Lacy.

Wentworth too would have known the Bladens since Robert Bladen was employed by the Savile family at the time when Wentworth's sister married into the same family and the two men (Radcliffe and Wentworth) spent a week residing at Thornhill during Robert Bladen's time of being employed by the Savile family. When Wentworth was appointed Lord Deputy of Ireland, he took Radcliffe with him and Radcliffe's presence in Dublin is likely to have been the reason for John Bladen (son of Robert) visiting Ireland in the

---

[1] Early Yorkshire Bladens by Karen Proudler, 2015, ISBN 978-0-9566831-6-8

summer of 1634.[1] This places both branches of the Bladen family in the same place at precisely the same time.

Sir George was very much involved in local matters in Alderman William Bladen's own backyard where, it was said, he "*stormed very much against the church-warden of St Warbre's [Werburgh's] parish in Dublin for presenting a Mass-house that was newly erected within four or five houses of the Castle gate, in which Masse was frequently said and he commanded the presentment to be cast forth of the court, and never could further endure the said church-warden".[2]*

Wentworth's ruthless administration and unpopular efficiencies in Ireland, however, made him disliked in some quarters, especially his confiscation of land owned by Catholics who held the majority (60%) of the land at the time. Wentworth, who was recalled to England in 1639, was appointed as the King's principal advisor and given the title Earl of Strafford in 1640. Perhaps above all, it was Wentworth's raising of an army in Ireland that alarmed those in the English Parliament the most and what he might do with it, in the King's name.

Later that year some of those powerful and well connected enemies he had riled in Ireland found a way to bring about Wentworth's downfall when the King was forced to recall Parliament (after 11 years of personal rule) and Parliament took the opportunity to call for his impeachment. Wentworth's suggestion to the King that the Irish army could be used to enforce his will either in Scotland or England was seized on by Parliamentarians. An impeachment charge failed but the plotting to bring about his downfall continued unabated and Parliament passed a Bill of Attainder in April 1641. The King eventually abandoned his support of Wentworth and signed the death warrant for his execution.

The execution of their former Lord Lieutenant sparked anxieties in Ireland. Allegiances were polarized between those Irish Catholics who would support King Charles (with his Catholic leanings) opposed to the English Protestant Parliamentarians who were defying the king.

---

[1] The Fairfax Correspondence: Memoirs of the Reign of Charles I, edited by George W. Johnson, Vol. II, 1848. Six letters from John Bladen to 1st Lord Fairfax
[2] Recusant History, Vol. 27, p172

Anticipating that the English would sanction an invasion of Ireland to suppress Catholicism and prevent an Irish army from intervening in England or Scotland's affairs, the Irish Catholic gentry land-owners pre-empted that possibility by plotting to overthrow the Protestant English rule in Ireland with the aim of securing more power and freedoms for Catholics in Ireland.

Far from placating parliamentarians, following Wentworth's death, the King had been forced to flee London to the relative safety of Yorkshire where he was less disliked (if not more popular). Ireland was in a crisis which had been exacerbated by poor harvests, rising rents, 30% interest rates and with the result that many land owners were heavily in debt. A plan was formed to take Dublin Castle[1] on 23rd October 1641 and other rebels were charged with seizing other locations. Ironically, the forming of these plots was hatched in Castle Street itself in Dublin, where Connor Maguire (one of the plotters who was subsequently executed for high treason) lodged, only yards away from Bladen's print shop.

Although the plan to take Dublin Castle failed, as news of the plan was leaked out, other places were taken and the general Catholic population was enthused by those successes. There were accusations of cruelty and brutality on both sides as the country became engulfed in rebellion. The workings of normal life in Ireland rapidly broke down as the State lost control in the face of the Catholic uprising and English Protestant settlers responded by raising their own militia for self-defence in Cork, Carrickfergus and Derry. Dublin too had its own militia which repelled rebel attacks with Sir Charles Coote being appointed the Governor of Dublin.[2]

The uprising beginning in October 1641 quickly spread and by the end of the year involved the whole of Ireland. William Bladen and his family, with the Bladen's bookshop and printing house located at Castle Street, were well placed to take advantage of the sanctuary Dublin Castle afforded them and, in a letter to his son, also called William and who was resident in London at the time, William Senior wrote to tell his son about the attempt to take Dublin Castle:-

---

[1] The population of Dublin in 1610, the time when the medieval map by John Speed on page 00 was created was only around 10,000

[2] Governor of Dublin, 1641, Sir Charles Coote, 1st Bt 1581-1642

1642[1] - "*Sonne, I have received your letter by Mr Portington, whereby I see you do not as yet understand how the case stands with us in this poor kingdom of Ireland which, that you may the better do, I will relate in brief.*

Beginning from the discovery of the plot to take the Castle and City of Dublin which should have beene the 23.October 1641 upon which day the rebels came to Master Arthur Champion's house,[2] some 60 miles from Dublin, where one of his own tenants came to him very early in the morning desiring to speak with him about some serious business, as he pretended, only to betray him when he had drawn him without the walls of his house (for he had a very strong house and well fitted for defence) had he known of their devilish treachery. Presently there came a company with two rogues which were pinioned as theeves, for stealing of his cattle. Master Champion bid them that brought them to carry them before the next Justice, for he would not meddle with them, whereupon these rebels set them loose and fell upon the good man, stabbed him with their skeanes to death presently, before he could give the least warning to those in his house. His brother, seeing many people there, went to see what the matter was. He was served in the same manner and a third likewise and then the rebels went into his house and killed two more, his wife and her sister and her brother-in-law. With two others that were in the house they took and keep prisoners to this day, taking possession of all they had, both within the house and without. She was downe upon her knees to beg a sheet to put her husband in for his buriall and another gentleman which came but over night with some other friends in love to visit him and the next morning lost their lives. And this they have done to many in those parts, robbing all the English Protestants, stripping them stark naked

---

[1] PB 365 Wood 507 (31 and 26) Ireland's True Diurnal. A True and Exact Relation of the Chief Passages in Ireland since the first rising of the Rebels. Sent by an Alderman of Dublin to his son now resident in London, Bodleian Library, Oxford. Jan 11. 1641/42

[2] Confirmed in 'Irish Rebellion of 1641 and the Wars of the Three Kingdoms' by Eamon Darcy, 2013, relating Viscount Arthur Chichester's account to the Secretary attending the King, Cal. State Papers Ireland, 1633-47, p342

and so turning them out to the fields and mountaines, in the frost and snow, whereof many hundreds are perished to death. They spare none, ministers nor people of what sort soever, they are so maliciously bent against us and our possessions that they will not spare our ministers bookes but burne and teare them in pieces. They destroy our English breed of cattell and sheepe in detestation of us, although one of ours is better than foure of theirs, and they have vowed to root out the name of the English out of this kingdome, and thus they goe on from the beginning almost all this kingdome over. And if the Lord in mercy prevent them not, it is like to bee so, for wee heare daily new rising of them in other places, which at first were quiet; as the County of Wicklow, all the Pale are out, notwithstanding their protestation in the Parliament there last meeting, which was since this rebellion begunne. Kings County and Queenes County rob and spoyl all.

The Good Lady, the Lady Offalia, and the Lord Digby's children and your brother are besieged in the Castle of Geshell. Having robbed them and all thereabouts without the castle these rebels have turned all the Protestants out of Kilkeny onely with the clothes on their backs by the Lord Mongaret, and keep the Countesse of Ormond prisoner. This Lord promised them a convoy to Waterford which went with them some eight miles out of towne and then left them, and a company of rogues met them and stripped them. When these poor people came to Waterford, hoping for succour, the towne would not suffer them to come in but keepe them starving without the towne. All the favour they shewed them they threw some bread over the wall, so that you may see how Waterford stands affected. These Rebels have great advantage of us, for they have their spyes daily with us, that nothing is said or done but they have notice presently sent to them; but we can have none to informe us of any particulars, for they meet with our spies, and hang them up with the rest of any English they meet with; and for that purpose have set up gallows 5 miles distant from one another.

At the first they spared the Scots, telling them their commission was onely to root out the English, but now they rob and kill Scots, not sparing any. One hundred and twenty they stript stark naked and *drove them upon a bridge and forced them into the water, drowned those which could not swimme and those which could swimme they knocked in the head when they came to land. Their cruell murdering of men before their wives to increase their griefe. Your brother writ unto me that a Rebell in those parts tooke an infant out of the mother's arms and cast it into the fire before her face; but the just judgment of God fell upon him, before he went from the same place hee brake his necke.*

The last week a Minister which came to this city left some goods with a supposed friend, sent for them, the goods could not be delivered unless he or his wife came for them, he would not go, she went, and when she came where the goods were they hanged her for her pains.

They rob close to this City: Beggarath, Cullens-wood, Ramynes [Rathmines], Phenix [Phoenix Park], Arntowne [Artane], Newtowne, Finglese [Finglas], Santry, Drumconfran [Drumcondra], Clantarffe, Hoth [Howth] all which border upon our City. Sir Charles Coute, our noble and brave Governour of this City sallied out one night and drave them from Clantarffe [Clontarf] and set it in fire. Another night to Sauntree [Santry] and another village and set them on fire: and the Earl of Ormond and Colonel Crafford, with Sir Charles Coote, drave them from Finglese [Finglas] and set it on fire. Sir Charles Coote and Sir Simon Harcotte sallied out to Swords, six miles from Dublin where the enemy had their camp and there had intrenched themselves. By break of day our men set upon them, drave them out of their Trenches and put them to rout, about 120 were slaine, divers taken prisoners, four of their Colours, drummes and arms our men brought away, who are safely come againe, blessed be God, onely we lost 4 men; whereof the chiefe was Sir Lorenzo Cary,[1] brother to the Lord Faulkland, shot in the head, as it is thought, by one of his souldiers; he was brought to Dublin on horseback, his footman behind him holding him up in the saddle, which an

---

[1] Attended St John's College, Cambridge in 1621 with his brother Lord Falkland

Irishwoman on the key seeing said it was pitty that no more were served so, which the souldiers hearing, in a rage threw the woman into the river where she was drowned. The Rebels have burned all the plantation Towns in the County of London Derry but Derry and Colraine stand out stoutly. The last night they went out towards the Mountaines beyond Tallow, and burnt two or three villages, whereby those Rebels should not have any shelter so near us, but when our men came, they ranne away, and would not abide above two shot, so that till we have supply from England and Scotland, no good is to be done with them whereby we may follow them to the full; notwithstanding many Papists or the Jesuits, Priests and Fryers, and say in plaine tearms they have beene the cause of all this, and no question to the contrary, the Lord in mercy convert or confound them.

We are all much bound to God for our Gracious King, the Honourable Parliament of England, the mercifull and pious City of London, and the whole Kingdomes of England and Scotland for their care and pitty upon us, although as yet we have but little help to this great worke, but of that which we have received we are much comforted, and we doe not doubt of the rest, which doth not a little strike to the hearts of our enemies as we heare, by this you may see in part our calamities; but blessed bee God, our Lords Justices and Councell have provided for this City, that under God we hope to bee as safe as you in London, and so wee hope of Drohedah where a worthy Governour Sir Henry Tichborne holds out valiantly, although the Rebells have made many assaults upon the Towne. Provision is sent by sea to Drohedah, and we trust in God it will be safely delivered to them, but if not, they will be hard bested, but if it please God to send us more strength, we make no question by Gods assistance but to cleer the passage by land to succour them.

These miseries are great, the Lord be mercifull unto us; but this is not all, the most of our rich men and great men are fled from us into England, and have carried their estates with them, they have not left one penny to succour the poore distressed stript people who are come hither for reliefe, whereof we have at this present near three thousand, besides many hundreds are starved to death since they came only with want, for we are not able to doe more than we doe, we do relieve them far beyond our abilities; for my own part I pay much weekly for billeting money, besides what I give to the poor, the rich being gone, left their houses without any help at all unto us, not so much as common charges for the safety of this City, but all lyeth upon the poorer sort. The Lord in mercy forgive them this sin, this great sin, that the blood of so many hundreds which have perished by want be not required at their hands. Thus with my prayers to God to bless you, I rest, your loving father W. Bladen.

If you think fit you may have this Relation Printed, for I have written nothing but the truth and I am ashamed to see so many false Pamphlets concerning the passages of Ireland printed at London."

The above letter, written on 11th January 1642 made brief mention of events at Drogheda which Bladen's next batch of letters[1] dated from 10th January through to 3rd February 1642 expands on. A first-hand account of the ongoing siege at Drogheda was included which had been written by Dean Nicholas Bernard[2] on 7th January 1642. Immediately after the letter, William adds to the story he is telling his son in the letter by bringing events up to date.

Dean Bernard's letter:

"I doubt not, but you have heard long agoe what our Condition is, and hath beene here this Moneth, or six weekes, Besieged with

---

[1] Bodleian Library, Oxford: WOOD 507 (31), Ireland's True Diurnall, or A Continued Relation of the cheife passages that have happened there since the 11th January unto this present Sent from an Alderman of Dublin to his Sonne now resident in London. As also a letter sent from thence by the Deane of Ardagh to a friend of his in Dublin. Published by the importunity of divers friends in London and for the truth thereof may give satisfaction to this Kingdome. London, Printed for William Bladen, and are to be sold by Richard Royston in Ivie-Lane, 1641
A True Coppy of a Letter sent from the Siege of Drohedagh the seventh of January 1641 from Deane Barnard to a friend of his in Dublin
[2] Dean Nicholas Bernard c1600-61 who had been ordained at St Peter's Church in Drogheda

8,000. If we may believe their owne reports, what plots have beene conspired within as without, would be too long to relate, but God his mercy hath hitherto delivered us, and turned all their counsells into folly, we have diligently sought him by fasting and humiliation, and he hath returned us good cause of thanksgivings. Wonderfull things have beene done for us, which ought to be had in remembrance, even that the times yet to come may praise the Lord.

Upon Saint Thomas his Eve we had an onset about midnight which such a shoute as I never heard the like, but were repulsed with the loss of many on their side, and not one of ours so much as hurt, yet at Saint John's Gate where they came, the hottest were the most naked, since that we have made some sallies out upon them with the like success this morning where we slew about 100, forced another 100 into the River where many of them were drowned, recovered 50 armes, fired the towne they were harboured in, and brought away some bootie.

Another time some 500 issuing out to secure the bringing in some Corne, being unexpectedly met with in a great fogge by a multitude, we killed about 300 whereof some were Captaines of good quality among them, and in all these and divers more was there, not one man of ours lost.

This Christmas we have kept solemnly two or three dayes of thanksgiving and have still more cause dayly, all we fear is a famine that we be not relieved from Dublin in time; yet we have victuals for a moneth longer, before which we are confident the State will not faile us. Where my wife and children are, I know not, but I trust God is with them, as he hath beene with us. This place and time hath been a school of much experience and hath let us know indeed what it is to put ourselves into the hands of God in whose we are yet, and I am confident will not deliver us up into the hands of our enemies. We doubt not of partaking of your prayers, as you have a share in ours. Thus in the midst of much imployment and being weary of writting other Letters, I have stole a little time to salute so good a friend, whom I have ever loved, forget me not to such as shall be desirous to heare of my welfarre. In hast I rest, your assured loving friend, N. Barnard, Drodedah, the 7th January 1641 [/1642]."

William Bladen's words now follow as he continued the narrative of events by describing to his son how the militia based at Dublin Castle rallied to Drogheda's aid ...

"Upon the next Mounday after, was provision sent to them, and came late to them the next day, but with much difficulty and danger of our men. Upon Monday the 10th of January 1641/42 the provision and munition for Drohedagh set sayle from Rings End and put in at Skerries and pilledged, and burnt that towne being a Rebellious place, and so past on for Drohedagh: where our men saw all along up in the shore as they sayled the enemie lie as thick as swarmes of Bees, when our men came to the harbours mouth to sayle up the River, the enemy played upon mightily with their Musket shot in the River, the enemy had sunck two Gabbards, and Chained them together onely on one side with a Cable rope, but our men by Gods providence and a high tide, and a good winde, got over the rope, and all came safe into the towne (blessed and ever blessed be our good God) where they were joyfully received.

That night the enemy made a breach into the towne through the wall in an Orchard that joyned to the wall, and ranckt their men in order before they were resisted, but before they proceeded much further our men came upon them so valiently, that they brake their rancks, made them fly some into houses to hide themselves, some into the River, where many of them were killed and many drowned, and those that hid themselves were found out and the hiders of them had their due deserts, but the breach in wall was presently made up and Sir Henry Tichborne, the Governour, a most valiant religious and courageous man, caused a bag-piper to goe upon the wall and play, as if it had been for victory on the Enemies side, upon which the rebells came to the gate like swarmes of bees, one cryed open the gate, and so it was but with great shot and small shot these rebels were so payd, that happy was he that could get away the furthest off from their hot entertainment, so that the gate was shut againe without any to presse in upon them. This was upon Tuesday night. Upon the Wednesday, which was the twelfth, our men came away for Dublin, but a pinnice falling upon the sands, not being well acquainted with the river upon a low water, it was on dry land in a woefull case, for the enemy made upon our men, both horse and foote: and women in such abundance, that our men had no hope of escaping, the fury of the enemy was so great, bringing with them on Carrs and horse backs, loads of Furrs to save them from our shots but those our men fired the rebels brought pickaxes to stricke holes into the pinnice, and got to it under the sterne, that our men could not come at them with there shot, but valiantly leaped over-bord to them upon the sands with there swords and layd them upon the sands to sleepe, and playd upon their great numbers with great and small shot that they made lanes amongst them of great length, both men, and womens heeles went up apace, and yet their number was so great that they would not leave off which went the Captain (whose name is Stutevile) saw their fury, bestowed Granados amongst them, by which they were so affrighted and torne, that with shame and great loss, they left the poore pinnis [pinnace] to waite for the tide, which when it came in upon the sands, the blood of those that were slain and hurt, dyed the water as red as blood, and blessed be God our men came safe away, and have landed here at Dublin, who have related unto us, this blessed providence of our ever blessed good God towards them and us, and brought with them from Drohedagh two rebells, which Sir Henry Tichborne sent by them that he had taken there, and are now in the Castle of Dublin with two Jesuits that came out of Spaine with ten barrels of Gun-powder for the enemy with divers letters to these Rebells, to incourage them, with assurance of assistance and provision of munitions from forraigne parts, which were taken at Youghall [Youghal] by the Earle of Corke and sent hither.

We heare the Rebells made another assault upon Drahedagh since our men came away upon the fourteenth in which 800 of them were slaine and repulst with disgrace, and the last weeke another with the like successe, but because it is uncertaine I will not write of it till I heare the truth of it. The Lord make us thankfull for his wonderfull mercies vouchsafed unto us. Oh that our hearts were inlarged to bless and praise his Holy name, for these wonderfull benefits which we have received, and that the Lord would be pleased to bless the meanes which our gracious King, and the pious Parliament, and City of London have manifested unto us: that the winds and the Seas would afford them that are ready to come unto us for we have great need of men, munition and mony and provision, a speedy passage. I am at 26 shillings every weeke charges upon Souldiers which are in this City for the defence of it, by reason that the rich are gone for England, the burden lyeth upon the poore, till the Lord send us money to pay the soldiers, victualls are very dear, for the enemy hath taken and keeps all from us, but we trust in God when we have strength that our armies may go out upon them, that some will be brought again unto us, but till then we doe not part with these we have to defend this city, which the Lord in mercy grant us, thus praying the Lord to bless you, I rest, your loving Father William Bladen. Dublin 26th January 1641/42".

In the following letter William Bladen makes mention of Carnew Castle having been under siege from the rebels for a long time. In fact, 160 Protestant settlers were under siege for 22 weeks by up to 1,000 Rebels. Eventually the lack of food forced those under siege to surrender where upon some were hanged but most were taken to Dublin.

"January the 27. 1641/42
The last night some of our horse sallied out to Racoule [Rathcoole], sixe miles from Dublin, where they met with five or sixe hundred of the Rebells, which made as though they would have stood to a skirmish, being the greater number by many hundreds, but proved otherwise, for our men slew eightie or one hundred of them, and the rest ran away, our men brought in some pillige of Cattle, sheepe and

swine and came all safe in againe, blessed be God for his gracious protection.

I writ of a report of late, onset of the enemie made upon Drohedagh which is yet Continued to be true, which was to be done this day sevennight, but the Rebels have cut of[f] all our passage by land, so that what we heare is by their own relation; which is that our men have given the enemie a great overthrow having slain one thousand five hundred men, whereof two were Lords and one that was of estate in Lands, better than some of the Lords in which as they themselves report, we lost not above sixe men, the Lord grant it may prove true.

This week our Lord Justices and counsel have committed to the Castle of Dublin Sir Nicholas White, Alderman Jones and Sedgrave of the Caberagh, all rich men, both for Lands and money and many in this Citie deserve the like, had they their due desert.

Carnow Castle [Carnew] hath bin long besieged by the Enemie and yet houlds out, but driven to a great strait but in hope to be relieved by a gentle woman which was in it, she being formerly acquainted with the chief of those Rebels, the plot was this, that she should goe forth to him with a complaint of their misery, not being able to indure it shee having a sister within the Castle in the like case, that if they might be freed, shee would be a meanes that the Rebells might take the Castle, of which they were glad to heare of shee propounded the way, which was, that should he send with her according to her directions, five or sixe of the chiefe which she would undertake to bring into the Castle, and the rest of be readie, that when the iron gate was opened for her to come in, these five or sixe should follow close to her and keepe the gate open till the rest were come in, all which was performed but with such a device which those in the Castle with her had devised with Iron Chaynes that when the few with herselfe were come in, they kept out all the rest, by which they in the Castle have got good prisoners into them to make their own Conditions for what they want, or to hange their prisoners over the wall which the Rebels will be verie unwilling of, they being prime men amongst them, these gentle wemen are of the

Rochfords, who have two brothers heer the one a Captain the other a Lieutenant, both of them valiant souldiers, good Commanders and true and faithful subjects.

This morning some of our Army, both horse and foote, marched with eight peeces to new Castle Lions [Newcastle-Lyons, south-west of Dublin] *seaven miles from Dublin, a town wherein are seven Castles in which the Enemie kept their campe, but before our Armie came to the towne the enemie were fled and had taken away with them all the pillige but our Armie marched forward to Nase* [Naas] *where the Enemie had another camping place five miles farther, but of their successe we yet heare no Certainty of. The Lord in mercie prosper them and send them a victorious and safe returne, of which we hope and pray for.*

This last night Captaine Scout, with his horse all vollenteers, went forth towards Clantorfe [Clontarf] *and returning about breake of the day to Drumcouran* [Drumcondra] *which is but a mile from Dublin, they were beset by the enemie, both horse and foote, to the number of five hundred and our men being not fortie, yet they come of[f] with honor not looseing one man nor horse.*

The good Ladie Offalie with the young Lord and your brother with the rest in that Castle, have bin driven to great distresse, by reason of two of her servants that would have betrayed them by a rope from of the wall, one night when he should have watcht went to the Rebells and tould them, how to cut of[f] the water from them in the castle, which was done, whereupon they in the castle were forced to put their lives upon it to sallie out, which they did and when they had slaine ten or twelve of the Rebells the rest fled, so that by Gods good providence they in the castle had libertie and opportunitie to relieve themselves not onely in water but in Corne which the Rebels had threshed for themselves, but none of their owne, those in the Castle burnt the houses and church, so as if they come againe there will bee no shelter for them: since I have not heard from them, for they cannot send to me, nor I to them, the enemie lying in such abundance betweene them and Dublin, the Lord in mercy looke upon us all."

42

"Dublin, the 3. Feb. 1641/42
This day our Army, blessed bee God, are safely returned home, where they have done good service in burning fifteen or sixteen Rebellious Towns and Castles which harboured the enemie and brought with them Cattell and other pillage, but the Rebells themselves fled before our Army came to them, onely one Castle where they discharged one and so ranne away. Wee have so many Papists and Spies on their part amongst us in this Citie that we cannot doe or intend to do any thing but they have present notice given them. The Lord in mercy remove them all, Amen. Your loving father
Dublin the 3. Feb. 1641/2"

William's son Dr Thomas Bladen was also trapped under siege some miles from Dublin at Geashill Castle and there is a description of his ordeal later in the book when Thomas is discussed.

The last batch of William's letters generally indicate an improving situation with the English Protestant militia raids out of Dublin Castle being largely successful, though Bladen makes no attempt to hide the barbarity of their attacks. The prospect of reinforcements, news of which had reached those under siege, arriving from England or Scotland with fresh supplies and armaments lifted the spirits of the besieged. As the King fled London for Yorkshire, an Adventurers Act was passed whereby in return for investing money with the government, investors would have the promise of land from dispossessed Irish Catholics. Both Dr Thomas Bladen and his cousin William Leggett were Adventurers.

William's final letters date from 22nd February 1642 (n.s.) through to 8th March and they describe the ferocity of fighting.[1]

---

[1] A True Diurnall, or a continued Relation of Irish Occurrences from the twelfth of Febr. To the eighth of March. Printed after a Coppy[1] that was sent from Mr. William Bladen of Dublin, to his Sonne resident here in LONDON: shewing what overthrows was given to the Rebells, and what good successe the Protestant party had; with a Relation of the late relief of Trohedagh [Drogheda]. Printed at London for William Bladen, and are to be sold by Francis Couls in the Old Baily, 1642

February the 12. 1641/42
This day the Lord Lambert marched out to the Dean's Grange five miles from Dublin (with some horse and foot) where were a great multitude of the Rebels who had great advantage of our men, both of the ground and great ditches which, at the first onset, showed some courage to fight. But after twice discharge the Rebels betooke themselves to their heeles, where our men slew many of them; and in one company we slew one Captaine, one Lieutenant and one Corporall, tooke 12 or 14 prisoners, one of which was a Commander, they had sixe colours but all fled.

February 14. 1641/42
This day here were hanged seven Rebells, and the eighth had the Rope about his neck upon the ladder, he made a Speech, that his life or death was worth nothing, but if his life might be spared, he would doe that service which should be worth a hundred of his life, or else let him suffer, upon which he was for this time preserved, to make tryall of his good service, which if hee did not perform, hee must go to the Gibbet from whence he came.

February 15. 1641/2
This day a Rebell one of their Commanders was brought in, who on the Sabboth before drinking with the rest of his wicked Companions, made a vow that the first English he met with whatsoever, he would kill and wash his hands in their bloud, which he did the next day meeting with a woman, but being neare Dublin, some of our Scots accidentally met with him and brought him to our City, and upon examination he confessed his cruell Murder, and this day he was hanged for the same, as hee justly deserved.

This day more provision and men are sent to succour Tredaugh, the Lord in Mercy send them safe to them. We heard that Sir Henry Tichborne sallied out of Tredagh, and tooke a good booty of Cowes, Corne and Hay, which we hope is true, but it came to us by the Popish Rebells, otherwise we cannot heare from Tredagh by land.

We heare that the Lord President of Munster hath recovered Clomell out of the Rebells hands, and hath hanged the Mayor, and two or three Aldermen of that Towne, for their Rebellion which is here credibly reported to bee true.

February 22.
This day we heare that the Lord of Musgra, and the Lord Rouch [Roche] are revolted from us, and joined with the Rebells in the County of Corke; and that our Lord President of Munster is forced to goe into Corke for his safety, but if there bee a supply of men and munition in Bristoll, as wee heare and hope there is, I doe not doubt (by the Lords assistance) but that they will bee supprest in a short time: Musgra and Rouch [Roche] have two ... Countries, and good Land, which I trust in God will be hereafter planted with true hearted English, it is a country of a large extent, land enough for many thousands. We heare that the Rebells have besieged the City of Cork, Kinsale and Bandonbridge, and it is to be feared so true: but our confidence is in our good God the Lord of Hosts. This day here is landed a second supply in strength both horse and foot: and we heare and hope of more coming, which by the gracious assistance of our good God, wee hope Ireland will be new moulded both in Church and Common-wealth.

February 23.
This day more men landed here, with whom one Colonel Brimigham, a popish Colonell came and landed but he was discovered, taken and committed to the Castle. This night some of our forces purposeth some exploits, the Lord in mercy prosper their enterprises, and send them safe returne with victory and honour.

February 24.
This day wee heare our men, some foot and horse went the last night to Kilcstone; and by the way found two of our Towne that went to give the enemy notice of their comming to them, which were both hanged, as

they justly deserved. This night our men returned back to Dublin (blessed be God) and have done good service; wee forced the enemy out of their Trenches, out of the wood adjoyning to the Castle; in which wood they had intrenched themselves, also took from them two Barrells of powder, and one Barrell of shot, with 500 weight of match, killed many of them that were without the Castle, but could not get the Castle, because wee had no battering Peeces there, but all that could not get into the Castle betook themselves to their heeles and ran away; onely such as were laid fast by death, and could not run away. And we hope to visite them ere long in another manner.

February 28.
This day our men are returned from victualling at Tredagh (blessed be God, and have had a good success) the enemy had made a mighty Chaine of Iron with Boats, which they had sunke in the River: but such as the gracious providence of our blessed God, that the night before our provision was to goe up, to send such a mighty Tide, which broke the Chain, so that it was no hindrance to our passage: they had placed three peeces of Ordnance upon the passage, but upon the discharge of our Pinnices the Rebels ran away from their peeces, and our men have taken the three peeces, and part of the Chaine. I saw the Chaine in the Castle of Dublin, which wanted no strength, but it was the powerfull worke of our good God, to whom let us ascribe all praise and glory to his blessed Majesty for ever.

I could write of many other passages, but because of the uncertainty of them I omit, for my desire is to write nothing upon uncertainty: for I am ashamed to see some things in print, as that of birds and apparitions in the ayre to be seen here at Dublin is most false. The news we heard of Sir Henry Tychborne issuing out of the Town of Tredagh is most certain, he brought above eighty Cowes, one hundred Sheep, Corne and hay, but with much difficulty: for the enemy beset him Front and Reare, yet blessed be God our men got into the Towne with their pilladge.

March the 3.

This night our men purpose to march out upon the enemy, the Lord in mercy prosper their intentions, and send them good success, and a victorious returne. They carry with them ten peeces, five small and five great, but my trust is in the Lord of Hosts the giver of all victory, whom we pray for his blessed assistance, and gracious protection. But of this event I will, God inabling me, write in my next: for the packet is to goe in the morning from hence.

This day we heare that our men at Bandonbridge did go out of the Town upon the enemy, and slew 105 of them, and the rest ran away. We lost not one man, onely one man shot in the leg, in which, as all other we may behold the gracious goodness of our good God towards us. We heare that Sir H. Tychborn the last week marched out of Tredagh, and slew many of the Rebells, the rest ran away, so that the Rebells have no hope to take that Towne. Sir Henry sent to the rebellious Lords of the Pale, that they should send in the Countrey to Market with provision, otherwise hee would send what he wanted, and take the rest from them. I heard it from a good hand, and I doubt not of the trust of it, for which the Lord make us thankfull, as for al of his wonderfull mercies towards us.

Your loving Father, William Bladen.   March 8. 1641".

The 1641 Rebellion in Ireland triggered Civil War in England and, as King and Parliament battled it out on the British mainland, Ireland endured many years of upheaval. It was not just a war between Catholics and Protestants in Ireland, Royalists were pitted against Parliamentarians and the Irish were set against the English, and even at times, against each other.

Meanwhile, in another letter to his younger son William, who had just that year been freed by the Stationers Company, Alderman William described[1] the plight of his eldest son Thomas who was at Geashill Castle.

---

[1] 27th January 1641 PB 365 Wood 507 (31) and Arch H.E. 108 (39), Bodleian Library, Oxford

Two servants of Lady Offaly had betrayed the family by going out of the castle to tell the rebels how to cut off the water supply which they subsequently did and those inside were forced to come out of the castle to procure water and supplies. Some 10 or 12 rebels were killed by the party but the castle occupants managed to obtain both water and corn to sustain them during the siege. At the time William wrote this letter he had not heard from his son in quite a while, there being swarms of rebels between them.

Shortly afterwards, William was elected Alderman of Dublin in the place of Sir James Carroll, deceased and seemed to take on increasing administrative roles in Dublin. In 1642, from his residence in Castle Street and along with Sheriff John Pue, he was ordered to take receipt of half the 'plate' owned by the people of Dublin as a means for raising money for the army's relief. Meaning that citizens were required to hand over their silverware to Bladen and Pue so they could mint a coinage (siege money) whilst Dublin was under siege to allow everyday transactions to occur. Bladen and Pue were to be joined by Gilbert Tongues and Peter Vandenhoven (goldsmiths) to assist with valuations.

William was able to resume his business later in 1642 where, on 15th July, he printed '*A Most Damnable and Hellish Plot Exprest in Ireland and England, Sent out of Rome to the Chief Actors of the Rebellion in Ireland, to Animate and Stirre Them Up*' which shows him making full use of his press for propaganda purposes to support the Protestant cause.

One of the Bladen family's neighbours in Dublin was Sir James Ware[1] b1594 in Castle Street, the son of French immigrants. Ware became Auditor-General and was a good friend of the Earl of Strafford who secured him a seat on Ireland's Privy Council. Ware published many works and was an accomplished antiquarian who made good use of his friend William Bladen's printing presses. He was, like William, present at the siege of Dublin and was a good friend of Lord Lieutenant Ormond. It was to be on a section of Ware's house and land at Castle Street/Austin's Lane where a new development was built called Hoey's Court.

---

[1] Ware made use of his neighbour William Bladen to publish some of his works. Sir James Ware (junior) has a sister called Cecilia who married "a" Dudley Loftus, William Bladen printed the works also for Dudley Loftus

The satirical author Dean Jonathan Swift was born there in 1667 and Swift's relations with the Bladen family is expanded on later in a separate section.

6. MAYOR OF DUBLIN

William Bladen's civic duties, which began in 1637 with his election as an Alderman, culminated in him becoming Mayor of Dublin.[1] On 29th September 1647, upon his father's election, William (the younger) who was present in Dublin for the occasion, petitioned the Dublin Assembly for £200 to support his father's mayoralty for the coming year.[2] The first point of business after William's appointment was to evict 28 members of the City Council who had supported the Irish in arms against Parliament.[3]

Under the Commonwealth there were stringent restrictions imposed on Bladen as sole printer in Dublin; he was required to submit a copy of anything he intended to publish before the Clerk of the Council for perusal first to ensure nothing derogatory was published against the Commonwealth. An order was issued stating *"That the printer in Dublin should not suffer his press to be made use of, without first bringing the copy to be printed to the Clerk of the Council; who, upon receiving it, if he found anything tending to the prejudice of the Commonwealth, or the public peace and welfare, should acquaint the Council with the same, for their pleasures to be known therein".*

William managed the transition from King's Printer to Commonwealth printer well enough, but suffered loss of support in his advancing years at the Restoration. Later, in 1661, during the backlash against anything connected with Cromwell's era, Parliament issued the following statement *"that all Bibles that had been printed by the late Usurper's Printer, calling himself Printer to his Highness the Lord Protector, should have the title-page where those words are printed torn from them; and that no sale be made within this kingdom*

---

[1] CARD II, pp449-50
[2] CARD, Vol.3, pp449-450, Dublin Record Office
[3] CARD, Vol.3, p38

of any Bible with the said title-page; but that new title-pages be printed by Mr John Crooke, His Majesty's Bookseller, whereof all booksellers are to take notice". This was as emphatic a snub to the Bladens as could be. Crooke had been appointed King's Printer at Charles II's Restoration and during the years following William Bladen's death in 1663, Castle Street in Dublin evolved more into a book-seller and printers' district as more and more printers were established and drawn to the area. Traders included John North in 1659, Samuel Danger in 1663, John Leach in 1666, Joseph Wilde in 1670, the Crookes and many, many others.

Other snippets of information about William in his later life include that in the 1650s his name appears as one of the congregation of Samuel Winter and he was also part of a committee that loaned money to the Commonwealth.[1] Irish State Papers show William being repaid £500 *"to those who have advanced money to the companies of the army".[2]* This is an interesting detail as William's son Dr Thomas Bladen later claimed that his father had loaned the King money and that he had been a Royalist supporter throughout. Thomas, in trying to change the perception of his father's loyalties, has to be seen in the context that he was desperately trying to regain the lost status as King's Printer, but the Bladens had been tainted by association with the Commonwealth and never regained it.

In 1653 William had been named as one of 12 persons constituting a committee formed to request large sums of money due to Dublin from the Commonwealth, whether they be paid by money or land. He was appointed, along with Alderman John Carberry, to repay funds to those who had contributed to the army's maintenance, the poorer individuals being the first to be repaid.

First wife Mary Young died some time before 7th February 1654 when William embarked on a second marriage to the widowed Eleanor Pemberton.[3] Eleanor must have been a lady of some considerable means because when William died, he mentioned certain properties that came to him through marriage to Eleanor which he returned to her disposal in his Will.

---

[1] CARD and the Church of St Werburgh Dublin by Rev S.C. Hughes, 1989
[2] State Papers, Ireland, dated 1st March 1642
[3] St Bridge, PRS, XI, 113. Eleanor appears in some records as 'Easter'

As well as their house in Sheep Street Dublin, there were also parcels of land at St Stephen's Green (called Flint's Park) and another piece of land near the Hogg and Butts. His own property was devised three ways: that is to say one-third to Eleanor, one-third to his eldest son Dr Thomas Bladen and the final one-third portion to the children of Dr Thomas Bladen. This estate included his print shop and warehouses both in Dublin and London and he also owned the house next door to the print shop which was rented out. His Will is reproduced in the Appendices on page 89.

During the 1650s William continued his print activities and bookselling and on 14th July 1657 records show he was paid £652-3s-6d and on 8th December 1658 he was paid a further sum of £531-2s-9d for some official printing. In 1660 he printed what became known as the earliest regular Irish periodical, 'Account of the chief occurrences of Ireland Nos 1-5'.[1]

Towards the end of the 1650s William and his family appear in a 1659 census of Ireland as being resident at St Werburgh's Street in Dublin; this seems likely to have been his private residence as the business continued at Castle Street. By this time he had lost his monopoly in official printing to John Crooke[2] of London, though he retained (or resurrected) use of the royal arms in 1660 and, at the Restoration, petitioned in vain for his title of King's Printer to be reinstated.

There is an account of William's activities after the siege years by his son Thomas in a 1681 letter to Archbishop William Sancroft, of which the following is a précis:

"He recites his, and his father's, record of loyalty to the King, and of the King's heavy arrears of indebtedness to him; and points out that his services and deserts have gone unrecognised. He desires no more than a good deanery on the occasion of Dr Sheridan's[3] forthcoming promotion to a bishopric. He describes that his father was the first of

---

[1] Wing, Serial 5

[2] A Dictionary of Members of the Dublin Book Trade, 1550-1800; based on the Records of the Guild of St Luke the Evangelist, Dublin. Mary Pollard, 2000

[3] William Sheridan 1635-1711, Dean of Down 1669-82 and Bishop of Kilmore and Ardagh 1682-91, Chaplain to Ormonde from 1665, attended TCD

all the court of Aldermen to declare, and to hazard of his life, for the King's restoration; for Sir Hardress Waller, having the King's castle and magazine in possession, threatened to burn the city unless they yielded to Oliver; but his father defied him and was unanimously supported and shortly after Sir H Waller was forced to yield up the castle and was made a prisoner".[1]

From Thomas Bladen's letter then it is clear that, though the crisis of 1641-42 passed, the difficulties in Ireland continued for many years whilst Civil War raged in England. Sir Hardress Waller,[2] who had fought against the Irish Rebels in 1641-42 in defence of Dublin Castle, subsequently went to England and joined the New Model Army and later returned to Ireland in 1650s as a Major-General for Cromwell. In 1659 he was in charge of a force that seized Dublin Castle in Cromwell's name and this is the incident that Thomas Bladen is referring to in the above letter. Thomas claimed that his father William was a loyal Royalist and was the first of the Alderman to take a stand in the King's name. William had served as the Mayor of Dublin in 1647-48 and his voice would indeed have had some authority.

Despite decades of upheaval during the 1640s and 50s, the Bladens remained in Ireland and both William and Thomas, father and eldest son, stayed there for the rest of their days though Thomas did spend some years preaching in England before returning to Ireland.

In his later years William contributed financially to the restoration of St Werburgh's church, being 1 of 25 subscribers, and was listed as the holder of pew number 45 in 1662.[3] The church was one of the most fashionable and best attended in Dublin until a chapel was built at Dublin Castle.

Not many years before he died, William lost the title of King's printer as on 31st July 1660 John Crooke of London was granted it. Bladen however, no doubt through the goodwill of his friends and contacts, continued to print for the State through to 1661 despite Crooke's protestations.

---

[1] IMC: Tanner Letters, 36, f158, dated 1681
[2] Sir Hardress Waller, c1604-66, regicide, Irish land owner, Governor of Cork
[3] CARD and 'The Church of St Werburgh Dublin' by Rev S.C. Hughes, 1989

Perhaps William felt that his loyalty to the King deserved the reward of restoring his printing monopoly to him. He never stopped trying to regain the title and on 29th April 1662 William petitioned Ireland's Lord Lieutenant claiming that he was owed £1,000 (son Thomas later claimed the figure was £2,000) for State printing and pleaded for the restoration of the patent as King's Printer. William claimed to have *"laid out his whole Estate in building a spacious printing howse and furnishing it with three printing presses and twenty sortes of Letters"*. He also complained that he was *"growne very old and decrepit, neare foure scoure years of age and much impoverished by the non-payment of the above sum"*. He was aggrieved that Crooke had *"a monopolie of printing and booke selling to the destruction of those trades and ruine of your petr* [petitioner] *and his wife and children and many families"*.[1] He never managed to have the debt repaid to him and also failed to regain the monopoly on printing.

Three days before he submitted the above Petition, William wrote his Will on 26th April 1662 and died one year later in July 1663 in Dublin, being buried at St Werburgh's Churchyard, inside the limits of the old city. His Will was proved that August and his second wife Eleanor outlived him until 1667 and received her husband's money, plate, jewels, brass, pewter, linen and all other household goods at his death. As previously mentioned, his estate was divided three ways between family members and he clearly wished his print businesses both in Dublin and London to continue as he gave directions that they were to be put into the hands of someone trained in the print business.

Mention was also made of his wife's daughter and made a bequest to his kinsman Jeremiah Rotherham[2] of Birmingham.

---

[1] NLI, MS 2511, Petitions to Ormond, Lord Lieutenant 1662-64, f24

[2] This bequest in Alderman William Bladen's Will "to his kinsman Jeremiah Rotherham of Birmingham" may help show a link between another branch of the family as there is a similar Will bequest from a Thomas Bladon, Vicar in Tamworth to his brother-in-law "Jeremiah Rotherham" and his administrator and cousin "Thomas Rotherham of Birmingham"

Jeremiah Rotherham,[1] as mentioned on page 23 (footnote 1) in this book, was a land agent who in 1677 was required to give a deposition in connection with a property called The Roundabout House in Birmingham[2] which stood at the junction between New Street and High Street in the town centre (demolished to make way for the Bull Ring).[3] This branch of the Bladen family descend from Alderman William's older brother Thomas. The Rotherams, or Rotherhams, may provide a link between the Bladens at Newton Solney, in that the previously mentioned John Rotheram who appears to have been a land agent for the Lords of the Manor of Newton Solney, was involved in the conveyance in 1599-1600 between William Bladen and his son-in-law William Goodriche when they sold off much of the family's land at Bladonfield to William Fitchett. The fact that we have another Rotheram (albeit in Birmingham) also involved as some kind of land agent and who, crucially, is mentioned in two Wills for Bladens in Newton Solney, is a strong indication of not only a continuity of Rotherham descent, but also of Bladens too. Jeremiah's deposition states that he had been *"gathering up all chief rents and other rents belonging to the Lord of the Manor in Birmingham ever since the year of our Lord 1641 ..."* For him to be a kinsman of the Newton Solney Bladens suggests he was perhaps a son, or even grandson, of the John Rotherham previously mentioned. Finally, William also made a bequest to his sister Anne and her two daughters.[4]

It is clear from his Will that William left well established businesses both in Dublin and London (where his younger son lived) and there remains the possibility that the emergence of a Samuel

---

[1] Jeremiah Rotherham, aka Jeremy Rotheram was a rent collector for Edward and Samuel Marrow, being the last Lords of the Manor of Birmingham. He gave a deposition on 3rd January 1676-77 concerning the rent collected from the Roundabout Houses. Birmingham Reference Library, ref 254558 (19/4)

[2] Victoria County History Series for Warwickshire, Vol. 7, Birmingham,

[3] The Roundabout Houses were demolished in 1769 when the Birmingham Street Commissioners were given permission to facilitate better access to the Bull Ring markets. The area is currently occupied by Waterstones and Next stores. A Short History of Birmingham from its Origins to Present Day by Conrad Gill, 1938 states that the churchyard of St Martin's was ringed in with buildings with were called the Roundabout Houses

[4] William Bladen: Arms, Fun.Ent. of Alderman Bladen of Dublin, d.1 Aug 1663 (or, three muscles in fess fleury gu. on a canton az. a chev. of the first)

Bladon as a printer in London a few years later was linked to this same family. Since it was William's son, William Junior, who was overseeing the London business then Samuel may well have been one of his offspring. Samuel and William (the younger) are discussed further on pages 84-85.

Karen Proudler

7. DR. THOMAS BLADEN

Alderman William Bladen's eldest son and heir Thomas was born around 1615 when the family's print business was becoming established at St Paul's Churchyard in London. His date of birth can be estimated from his later admission records at Trinity College in Dublin.[1] Thomas married at least three times:-

Dr Thomas Bladen D.D. c1615-95

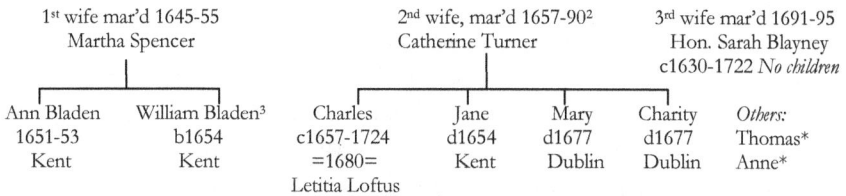

1st wife mar'd 1645-55 Martha Spencer		2nd wife, mar'd 1657-90[2] Catherine Turner				3rd wife mar'd 1691-95 Hon. Sarah Blayney c1630-1722 *No children*
Ann Bladen 1651-53 Kent	William Bladen[3] b1654 Kent	Charles c1657-1724 =1680= Letitia Loftus	Jane d1654 Kent	Mary d1677 Dublin	Charity d1677 Dublin	*Others:* Thomas* Anne*

* Thomas and Anne were children residing with Sarah Bladen (née Blayney)[4] in London in 1695. Since Sarah was a Blayney spinster at the time of her marriage to Dr Thomas Bladen, it is assumed she had no children of her own and so it seems likely that Thomas and Anne were younger children of her deceased husband Thomas Bladen.

By 1626 his father William had taken the family to Dublin, however it is possible that the Bladen's bookshop in London was maintained by a third party during the family's absence as there are frequent records of journeys by family members to and from Dublin

---

[1] Alumni Dubliniensis, Records of TCD

[2] Marriage of Thomas Bladen and Catherine Turner on 17th March 1657 at St Michan's Church, Dublin. See also the parish register of St John the Evangelist, Fishamble Street in Dublin, where Thomas and his family lived, records the burial of 'Madam Bladen, wife to Dr Bladon' on 8th August 1690

[3] Parish Register of 1654, Medway Archives and Local Studies Centre, P296/11, also Register of the Parish of St John the Evangelist, Dublin, 1619-99, edited by James Mills

[4] Hon. Sarah Blayney, 4th daughter of Henry 2nd Lord Blayney, Baron of Monaghan by the Hon. Jane Moore, daughter of 1st Viscount Drogheda

through the years. It is also known that William's younger son, William, was in London and trading as a bookseller.

As can be seen on the map on page 67, Dublin Castle and the Bladen business premises were very close to Trinity College and so the decision for Thomas to attend there from 1631-37 was probably an easy one.[1] He graduated from Trinity in 1638.

During the Irish Rebellion in 1641 Thomas, like his father William, was trapped under siege. In his father's case, as previously mentioned, William was trapped in Dublin Castle, Thomas was trapped at Geashill (referred to as Geshel in letters) Castle in County Offaly, about 50 miles to the west of Dublin with the Digby family.[2] It is not clear why he was attending the family at this time, possibly he was the family chaplain or he may have been friends with Essex Digby, son and heir of the family, who attended Trinity at the same time as Bladen.

Amongst letters kept by Alderman William Bladen, there is an account of how Thomas Bladen and the Digby family came to be trapped inside the Geashill castle walls. William related that a group of rebels,[3] led by Henry O'Dempsey, wrote to Lady Offaly, the lady who owned Geashill and who was the wife of Lord Digby: *"To the Honourable and thrice virtuous Lady, the Lady Digby these give. Honourable, Wee, his Majesties loyall subjects, being at the present employed in his Highnesse Service for the taking of this your Castle, you are therefore to deliver unto us free possession of your said Castle, promising faithfully that your Ladyship, together with the rest in the said Castle restant, shall have a reasonable composition; otherwise upon the not yielding of the Castle, we doe assure you that we will burne the whole Towne, kill all the Protestants and spare neither man, woman nor child upon taking the Castle: consider (Madam) of this our offer and impute not the blame of your owne folly unto us, think not that here we brag, your Ladyship upon submission shall*

---

[1] A Dictionary of Members of the Dublin Book Trade, 1550-1800; based on the Records of the Guild of St Luke the Evangelist, Dublin, Mary Pollard, 2000; Alumni Dubliniensis, Records of TCD

[2] Lettice Fitzgerald, 1st Baroness Offaly c1580-1658 married Sir Robert Digby

[3] The rebels were: Henry Dempsy, Charles Dempsy, Andrew Fitzpatrick, Conn. Dempsy, Phelim Dempsy, John Vicars and James McDonel

have a safe convoy to secure you from the hands of your enemies and to lead you to where you please, a speedy reply is desired with all expedition and thus we surcease".[1]

Lady Offaly replied defiantly:[2] *"I received your letter wherein you threaten to sack this my castle, by His Majesty's authority. I have ever been a loyal subject, and a good neighbour among you, and therefore cannot but wonder at such an assault. I thank you for your offer of a convoy, wherein I hold little safety, and therefore my resolution is, that, being free from offending His Majesty, or doing wrong to any of you, I will live and die innocently, and will do the best to defend my own, leaving the issue to God. And though I have been and still am desirous to avoid the shedding of Christian blood, yet, being provoked, your threats shall no wit dismay me ...."*

Although Lady Offaly (widow of Sir Robert Digby) stood her ground, she nonetheless later wrote to the Earl of Ormonde in 1641/2 advising him she had been besieged by the Dempseys for 16 days. She described how, but for the Grace of God sending rain, they would have all perished for lack of water but that the rebels *"they have taken all my sheep, cattle and horses and set fire of all my winter provision for firing and now I remain as a prisoner within these walls which they threaten to batter about my ears"*. She begged him for assistance. Her call for help was heeded and Sidney, Viscount Lisle, Lieutenant-General of the Horse in Ireland was despatched to assist her. She remained at the castle until October of that year but returned to England at this time after further threats by Charles O'Dempsey. The castle, however, remained in the hands of Sir Richard Grenville who was in Viscount Lisle's service.

In the aftermath of the initial rebellion, Thomas moved away from Ireland for a decade, though he made frequent visits there.[3]

---

[1] Bodleian Library Oxford, WOOD 507 (26), also a Letter of the Rebels, subscribed with divers of their hands, written to the Lady Offalia, mother to the Lord Digby, to deliver up her Castle of Geshel, she with the Lord Digby's children and others being therein. With her resolute and modest Answer thereunto

[2] Account written by Lord Frederick Fitzgerald published in the County Kildare Archaeological Society Journal, Vol. V, No. 3 (1899-1902)

[3] CSP 1642-59 ref Adventurers. List of Adventurers for the barony of Tuteraux Co Armagh, North-West Quarter: John Shepherd, Thomas Bladen and Maurice

From 1645 Thomas, who was now a Doctor of Divinity,[1] resided in England where he had secured himself a position at St Margaret's Church[2] in Rainham, Kent.[3] By 1650 he was married to Martha Spencer[4] and the couple began their family shortly afterwards with daughter Anne being baptised on 27th May 1651 at Rainham.[5] Thomas maintained his interest in Ireland, however, during his time in Kent and there are various records of his involvement in land acquisitions in Ireland for himself and relations. In 1653 he arranged for a bond for Richard Young of Lombard Street, London (a mercer); this is most likely a member of his mother's family. The bond was for £200 to Protector Cromwell in respect of John Young's subscription to the Irish Adventure.[6] Similarly Thomas was involved with his cousin William Leggett[7] in a draw for a lot of land in Armagh.[8] All these schemes were methods of raising money to finance the Parliamentary cause,[9] but were done with the promise of

---

Thompson. 1643 (actually the loans were spread over 1632, 1642 and 1647)

[1] Records of the Church of England Clergy Database: Bladen, Thomas, 25 March 1645,office/status Vicar, location Rainham, Kent Source PRO E331 Canterbury/12 Returns to First Fruits Office. Ordinary / Jurisdiction. Patron type: Crown. Gender male. Patron surname: King Charles. See also Lambeth Palace Library records: COMM I/46, I/99 and I/100

[2] A Dictionary of Members of the Dublin Book Trade, 1550-1800; based on the Records of the Guild of St Luke the Evangelist, Dublin, Mary Pollard, 2000

[3] Rev. Alan Vousden (2002) of St Margaret's Rainham confirmed Thomas Bladen's name is displayed on a board in St Margaret's of past incumbents from 1645-56. At the time Rainham was in the diocese of Canterbury with an expansive geographical area but a small population of 300, now Rainham is in the Rochester diocese with a population of 30,000+

[4] Marriage on 8th August 1650 at St Peter-le-Poer, London

[5] Original parish register, Kent

[6] CSP: 1642-59 Adventurers

[7] CSP: 20th January 1654, Ireland refers to William Leggett being a cousin of Thomas Bladen and that Thomas was minister of Raynham, Kent and his cousin William Leggett was to draw his lot for a barony in Armagh. This was probably William Leggett, Presbyterian Minister at Dromore from 1675-95 who was a senior figure in the Presbyterian Church, teaching divinity to students. Testimonial of John Leask, Bodleian Library, MS Carte 221, p275. He resided briefly at Fenwick and attended Paisley from 1689 to 1691, after which time he returned to Ireland. Thomas Blackwell's The New Statistical Account of Scotland, Vol. VII, Renfrew - Argyle. 1845

[8] State Papers Ireland, 20th January 1654

[9] A Dictionary of Members of the Dublin Book Trade, 1550-1800; based on the Records of the Guild of St Luke the Evangelist, Dublin, Mary Pollard, 2000

a return in land allocations in Ireland,[1] that is to say, the Adventurers were promised land which would have been taken from Catholics.

Other children were born and died whilst Thomas and Martha were residing at Rainham. The death of a daughter Jane occurred in 1654[2] along with the birth of a son William on 25th May of that year.[3] year.[3] After almost ten years at Rainham in Kent during the most turbulent years of the English Civil War, Thomas decided to return to Ireland and in 1654/55 he was appointed Commonwealth Minister of Duleek[4] (just north of Dublin) at a salary of £100 per year.[5] A record dated 16th May 1655 shows a pass being issued for "for Thomas, son of Mr Bladen, merchant of Dublin, with wife, mother, child and servant to Ireland". It is not known if the mother referred to is Thomas's mother or his mother-in-law and shortly after this Martha had died and Thomas's own mother (Mary Young) was also deceased. A further record for 24th January 1656[6] shows Thomas again making the journey to Ireland though no family was listed as being with him so he was probably travelling alone. Approximately two years after wife Martha's death Thomas married Catherine Turner on 17th March 1657 at St Michan's Church in Dublin and the following year he had a son Charles.[7]

---

[1] A Little History of Ireland by Martin Wallace, 1994

[2] Scans of original parish registers for St Margaret's of Antioch's, Rainham, Kent, courtesy of Medway Council, www.cityark.medway.gov.uk

[3] Ibid

[4] A Dictionary of Members of the Dublin Book Trade, 1550-1800; based on the Records of the Guild of St Luke the Evangelist, Dublin, Mary Pollard, 2000. See also Analecta Hib. 15 (1994)

[5] Records of the Church of St John the Evangelist, Dublin

[6] Ibid

[7] According to George Thomas Stokes in Some Worthies of the Irish Church, "by his first wife Dr Dudley Loftus had several children, one of whom alone lived to be married. She was Letitia, who married Mr Bladen, the son of William Bladen, king's printer here in Dublin all through the reigns of Charles I, Cromwell and Charles II". Stokes, however, was incorrect in that it was William's grandson Charles (son of Dr Thomas) who married Letitia Loftus - see depositions under the section for Loftus-Bladen marriage and Bunbury v Bolton

He was appointed Minister of Drogheda in 1658[1] and, two years later, he became the Prebend of Dunlavin at St Patrick's Cathedral which was an appointment he was to hold for six years. This was the same appointment which would later be held by the author Jonathan Swift who had quite a poor opinion of Bladen, which will be discussed later.

His presence in Dublin facilitated Thomas Bladen's involvement in his father's print business and bookselling which he continued long after his father's death, combining it with his ministry.[2]

On 27th June 1662 Thomas became Rector of Kilskyre, Killallon and Diamer (Barony of Fowre) and Grilly (Meath).[3] In addition, three three months later on 28th August of that year he was appointed by James, Duke of Ormond, to be one of His Grace's Domestic Chaplains in Ordinary.[4] Ormond[5] and his family had just returned from exile and had been reinstated to their titles and lands following the Restoration of King Charles II. Among the many titles conferred on him by a grateful king, he was made Lord Lieutenant of Ireland. Ormond was one of the highest profile figures in Ireland at the time and the appointment of Thomas as his Chaplain must have been quite a feather in Bladen's cap.

Later that year his father William wrote his Will and died a few months later. This meant that Thomas was now in charge of the printing business,[6] at least he was nominally in charge because he had had Nathaniel Thompson[7] and Josiah Windsor[8] to manage the business on a day-to-day basis.[1]

---

[1] A Dictionary of Members of the Dublin Book Trade, 1550-1800; based on the Records of the Guild of St Luke the Evangelist, Dublin, Mary Pollard, 2000. See also St Michan, PRS, III, p56

[2] Irish Records Index 1500-1920

[3] Alumni Dubliniensis, Records of Trinity College

[4] Oxford University's Bodleian Library Special Collections, Notification or Signification dated 28 Aug 1662 of Thomas Bladen's ordinance

[5] James FitzThomas Butler, 1st Duke of Ormonde 1610-88

[6] A Dictionary of Members of the Dublin Book Trade, 1550-1800; based on the Records of the Guild of St Luke the Evangelist, Dublin, Mary Pollard, 2000

[7] Literary, Political, Scientific, Religious and Legal Publishing, Printing and Bookselling in England 1551-1700. Nathaniel Thompson was not a native Englishman. He was born in Ireland, probably In Dublin, about 1648. At the age of 15 he was apprenticed to William Bladen." Thompson produced books in 1665-66 for Thomas Bladen including Praxis Francisci Clarke

[8] A Dictionary of Members of the Dublin Book Trade, 1550-1800; based on the

In 1664/5 Thomas secured an appointment as Dean of Ardfert[2] after failing earlier in 1664, on 12th January, in an attempt to regain the title as King's Printer. For ten long years he would try to regain the monopoly[3] and, in 1671, this culminated in the Dublin Council issuing a prohibition notice to him, preventing him from doing any printing, or even make use of his press.

Clearly Thomas took no heed of the Council's Order because on 8th September 1673 yet another 'Final Order' was issued to Bladen demanding the cessation of printing activities and the Order[4] sought the removal of all Bladen's materials used in the printing process.[5] It is doubtful that this Order had any impact on him because as late as 1681, Thomas was still involved in the book trade having imported 2.5 cwt of books from Chester.[6] They could, of course, have been for his private use but given the family's history as booksellers it seems more likely to have been a defiant restocking exercise.

In 1677 Thomas suffered a double blow when two of his daughters died within weeks of each other. Mary died on 8th August and Charity Bladen on 20th December 1677[7] and, although their causes of death cannot be known, it could be speculated as being spotted fever (typhus). Both daughters were buried at St John the Evangelist Church in Dublin.

---

the Records of the Guild of St Luke the Evangelist, Dublin, Mary Pollard, 2000. Josiah Windsor in 1667-9 produced three books under the management of Thomas Bladen including a couple by Dudley Loftus, including 'William Penn's Great Case of Liberty of Conscience Once More Debated' in 1670

[1] A Dictionary of Members of the Dublin Book Trade, 1550-1800; based on the Records of the Guild of St Luke the Evangelist, Dublin, Mary Pollard, 2000

[2] Alumni Dubliniensis states this appointment was the following year, on 6th April 1666

[3] Order in Council attempting to forbid others from engaging in printing NLI, MS(G) 16998, p224

[4] MS 16998, pp183-6 and 193

[5] Ibid

[6] A Dictionary of Members of the Dublin Book Trade, 1550-1800; based on the Records of the Guild of St Luke the Evangelist, Dublin, Mary Pollard, 2000

[7] Registers of the Parish of St John the Evangelist, Dublin, 1619-99

Fishamble Street, Dublin

Early census records show that in 1659 Thomas was a resident of St Werburgh's parish and by 1680 the Pipe Water Accounts[1] show him living at 14 Fishamble Street in the centre of Dublin close to the Bladen Bookshop on Castle Street. This property was just a few doors away from No. 20 Fishamble Street where later, in 1742, the first performance of Handel's Messiah took place at a music hall. Just a short distance away from the Bladens' house, which was called Glebe House (and was probably a parsonage provided for Thomas as a member of the clergy), there was the church of St John the Evangelist which had been rebuilt in 1681. Vestry records show that Thomas Bladen had several quarrels with those in the vestry at the time and the Bladen name shows up as occupying one of the 42 pews in the church. Thomas was the Prebend of St John's right through from 1660 to his death in 1695.

Other activities for Thomas at this time include his 1680 possession of a monument of Lord Roper in St John's Church,[2] as settlement for an outstanding debt. The incident appears to have taken place when St John's Church was in a poor state and about to be pulled down. He also acquired or purchased, for a period of three years, *"the tithes great and small of the parsonage of Killaleagh in the Diocese and County of Meath at a rent of 70 l. Sterling".*[3] Shortly afterwards mention was made of Thomas in a letter dated 29th December 1681 from John Graham to the Bishop of London and in 1690 the parish records indicate that Thomas's wife died, *"death of Madam Bladen."*[4]

---

[1] Vol. VII of the Book of Irish Families, Great and Small by Michael C. O'Laughlin, President I.G.F., Editor, Irish Family Journal, 1999

[2] Church Monuments: Journal of the Church Monuments Society, 1996

[3] Report of the Royal Commission on Historical Manuscripts: Issue 9

[4] Registers of the Parish of St John the Evangelist, Dublin 1619-99

8. DIFFICULTIES

Swift

Jonathan Swift, satirist and author of Gulliver's Travels, grew up in the shadow of Bladen's print shop as the Swift family lived at 7 Hoey's Court in an area immediately in front of Dublin Castle. Hoey's Court was connected to Castle Street by a passageway called 'Cole's-Alley'.

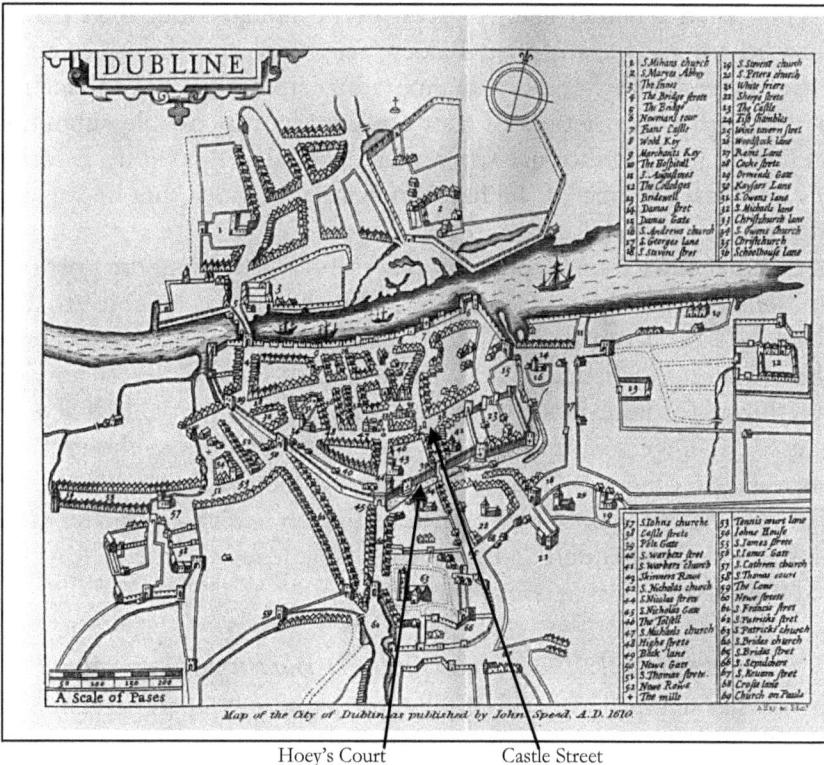

Hoey's Court   Castle Street

Although there was many years difference in age between Dr Thomas Bladen and Dr Swift, Swift seems to have been familiar with the Bladens and held the son Thomas in contempt.

Records of St John the Evangelist Church on Fishamble Street show both Bladens and Swifts in attendance and no doubt Swift family members attended when Bladen was ministering. Both men were correspondents of William King (Bishop of Derry, later Archbishop of Dublin) for long periods of time though, in Bladen's case, it seems more in an official capacity when he was rebuked for insufficient sermon making.

A particular incident occurred in 1681 which may have contributed to Swift's poor opinion of Bladen when Ezekiel Hopkins, the Bishop of Raphoe, moved to Derry and there was therefore a vacancy. Despite Bladen being well into his sixties and Swift being only in his teens, it does seem that the events surrounding the appointment of this bishopric resonated with him, even at such a tender age. At least two candidates put their names forward for the vacant post, Bladen being one and the other being Dean Peter Manby. Bladen attempted to strengthen his application by having a raft of letters of support from worthy people submitted endorsing his application.[1] Unfortunately Bladen slipped up by using his own seal on each of the letters making it obvious that he was the instigator of them all.

Neither Bladen or Manby was successful in obtaining the post but, in Manby's case, this caused so much bitterness that he converted to Roman Catholicism in disgust. His reasoning was that he believed there was more chance of advancement with King James II now on the throne for ministers within the Catholic church. Manby's actions caused a huge controversy at the time and it is thought he encouraged others to follow his path. Whether that included Dr Thomas Bladen is not known, though Bladen was called in later years 'some time independent'. This seems likely to be the incident which led to Jonathan Swift's comments:

Quid obstat, Dii boni, quominus Dr Bladen fiat Episcopus
What stands in the way, good God, let it be done to prevent
Dr Bladen [as] Bishop.[2]

---

[1] IMC: Tanner Letters, 36, ff135, 149, 158, 202, Early Modern Letters Online
[2] The works of Jonathan Swift, Vol. 6 by Sir Walter Scott, 1824

In the course of his futile letter-writing in 1681, Thomas signed his letters as 'Minister of St Andrew's in Dublin'. This was the Church of Ireland's parish church which was rebuilt after Cromwell's time to be located inside the city walls near Thingmote, close to Trinity College. The present-day St Andrew's Church on Andrew Street was re-built long after Bladen's time.

Thomas Bladen's second wife was buried in August 1690 and just a few months prior to that Thomas had received letters from William King complaining that he was neglecting his pastoral duties. The correspondence that has survived is only one-sided showing Thomas Bladen's response but his comments and spirited defence of his actions make it obvious that the archbishop had complained. The following are extracts from Thomas's letters:-

2ⁿᵈ May 1690

To the Reverend Mr King, Dean of St Patrick's Dublin[1]

"Sir, I was always for dayly prayers in ye church provided the parishioners did procure a reader at their own charge, for my curate hath by contract undertaken yt burden of which St Paul says who is sufficient for these things, he is to visit ye sick every day and to baptize and bury very often and to read prayers twice and preach twice on ye Lord's Day and to read prayers twice on Holy Days, all which is work enough for one man and when you understand ye rubrick you will not say yt it requires positively prayers every day but conditionally and ye canon expounds ye rubrick in saying positively yt prayers shall be read every Lord's Day and every Holy Day; and ye true meaning of ye Rubrick is yt prayers shall be read every day in Cathedral Churches, but you never knew prayers required by any lawful authority in parish churches every day. I am, your affectionate friend and humble servant, Tho: Bladen."

A few days later, Thomas expanded on his theories to William King:-

---

[1] TCD: MS 1995-2008, f74b, 75, 76, 76a dated 1690

5th May 1690

To the Reverend Mr King, Dean of St Patrick's Dublin

"*Yours I received this morning and I return you many thanks for your great pains in my concern. I know it is my duty to officiate as far as I can, though I have a curate, but I have been involv'd so much in debt by defending myself against fals reports in Chancery and by reversing unjust decrees grounded upon these fals reports (wch are upon record and proved to be fals upon record) yt from ye time I contracted with Mr Bunbury to this day durst not appear in publick , but I hope within a few weeks I shall overcome all my troubles and be able (by God's help) to perform all yt ye Rubrick injoyns without the help of a curate. And I say again yt which you understand ye rubrick you will not say yt it doth positively injoyn prayers publicly every day in ye week but then only when ye deacon is at home and not hindered reasonably. You have not a wife and children and therefore you have no reason to be busied in providing a maintenance for a family, but they yt have familys to provide for due find yt they are busy every day so much in providing for their family, yt they have not time enough to prepare their sermons unless they toil till midnight about their study .... according to the true intent of ye Rubrick which is more plainly express'd in yt Common Prayer Book printed in ye reign of King Charles the First Anno Domini 1638 ye words whereof are these following: all priests and deaconry shall say dayly morning and evening prayers either privately or openly except they be let by preaching, studying divinity or some other urgent cause.*

Do you think yt an ordinary divine is able to preach twice every Lord's Day and visit the sick every day and many times all day long and to provide food for his family and yet to read prayers publicly every day. Our forefathers did never think it, and therefore never preached it but in cathedrals only and there is room enough in cathedral churches to receive all ye frequent public prayers every day.

I know for the present Christchurch is taken from us, until it be restored we are bound to see that all who frequent public prayers be not disappointed but for any single person to continue reading prayers in parish churches while the cathedral churches are open is but ..... for which sin God hath threatened to take his word from us. I have read prayers on holidays when there was no more in ye church than myself, clerk and sexton, so yt ye Papists have looked down upon us and despised our religion.

What a sad confusion should we be in if at ye same time when ye people are call'd to church ye priest or deacon should be call'd away to baptise two or three dying infants or to attend a corpse to the grave or to joyn a couple in matrimony, which accounts due often come to pass.

I wish with all our praying and preaching we could prevail with ye people to read prayers in their familys every working day rather than to go to public prayers and leaving their familys starving at home for want of prayers. I know some familys who thus understand ye Rubrick and yt point of praying privately, yt is in their familys not in their closets only, your Lord Christ who has exalted us to pray in our closets gives us no other direction to guide us ...."

Bunbury

Thomas referred, in the above letter, to a dispute with 'Bunbury' in the first paragraph as the reason for him not appearing in public. Although he made no mention of the man's Christian name, it seems likely that he was referring to Walter Bunbury 1664-1749 of Moyle (son of Thomas Bunbury of Ballyseskin in County Wexford). Why the two were in dispute over a contract is not known, though it is difficult to imagine that Bladen's pastoral ministry would have been the problem, perhaps rather it was a dispute connected with Bladen's printing and book-selling business. Whatever the nature of their dispute in 1690, the name Walter Bunbury cropped up again in dispute with Bladens some years later, between the same Walter Bunbury and the son of Dr Thomas Bladen. This will be discussed in the next section 'Loftus-Bladen Marriage'.

Not long after his second wife's death, Thomas embarked on his third and final marriage to Hon. Sarah Blayney[1] on 28th July 1691 at St Martin-in-the-Fields Church in London.[2] Thomas was well into

---

[1] Musgrave's Obituary ref Sarah Bladen (nee Blayney)
[2] Marriage licences issued by the Archbishop of Canterbury, "Marriage of Revd

his seventies when they married and Sarah was perhaps around sixty and well past child-bearing age, so there were no children from the union. Sarah was a descendant of Adam Loftus and had a good fortune of her own which she was able to dispose of as she pleased, since she outlived Thomas by many years to 1722.

In his final year, 1695, Thomas edited and published Clarke's Praxis (a celebrated law treatise from 1596), showing he continued his involvement with printing right to the very end.[1] He was also reported to have delivered a sermon on 2 Cor.VI-On Rev. XV3-on Ezek, xxxiii84 in 1695.[2] He was buried on 4th July 1695 at St John the Evangelist Church in Dublin.[3] This was the same church his second wife had been buried in, as too were his daughters Charity and Mary in 1677 who were buried "in ye church".

Thomas Bladen, Dean of Ardfert in Ireland, (above 50) and the Hon. Sarah Blayney (above 30)"

[1] The Lives of the Professors of Gresham College. A celebrated law treatise, Clarke's Praxis, "which tho written for the use of students and advocates in the year 1596 and as the editor of it Dr Bladen sais in his dedication, *per 70 annos praetor propter decorous magno in pretio babitus*, [for 70 years he was held in high esteem decorous habit] had never been printed, till it was then done by him; when the text was so corrupted by frequent transcripts, that he found it difficult to restore either the sense or language"

[2] The Fruits of Endowments: a list of works of authors who have, from the Reformation, Enjoyed Prebendal or other Non-Cure Endowments of the Church of England by F.R.A. Glover, 2012

[3] Registers of the Parish of St John the Evangelist, Dublin, 1619-99, p245

9 . LOFTUS-BLADEN MARRIAGE

There has been speculation through the centuries about a Loftus-Bladen marriage; that is to say, not that such an event took place, but rather who the specific Loftus and Bladen individuals were. The two families lived close to each other in Dublin and were related; Alderman William carried out printing for members of the Loftus family and Dr Dudley Loftus attended Trinity College Dublin at the same time as Dr Thomas Bladen. After the marriage of Dr Dudley Loftus's daughter to Dr Thomas Bladen's son, the two families were even more closely connected and after the death of his first wife Loftus made use of his friend Bladen, who was Prebendary at St John the Evangelist Church in Fishamble Street, to conduct the service for his second marriage to Lady Elizabeth Ervin [Irwin] on 11th May 1693.[1]

Even contemporaries had their wires crossed on this marriage as a manuscript at Trinity College Dublin, prepared by Dr John Madden (President of the College of Medicine/Physicians, and a Manuscript Collector) in 1703 incorrectly stated that "*a Bladen married Jane Loftus*".[2] On the Loftus side, it was known to be a daughter of Dr Dudley Loftus (now identified as Letitia) and poor Letitia has been endlessly speculated about as to which Bladen she married, with different authors arriving at different conclusions and creating plausible reasons why. She married, in fact, Charles Bladen[3] who was a son of Dr Thomas Bladen.[4]

---

[1] Will of Elizabeth Bunbury, commonly called Dame Elizabeth Irwin, formerly Broughton, TNA: PROB 11/804/474 probate 16th November 1753

[2] TCD: MS 1213 Dr Madden, 1703

[3] Although Charles Bladen left a Will in Ireland in 1724 the records have been lost/destroyed. Charles Bladen subscribed to The General History of Ireland, D O'Connor in 1723

[4] Bunbury v Bolton Chancery Case. Madden's manuscript records the initials B.A. after the Bladen name but, since he had the wrong individuals identified this cannot be given much credence

The source of this new information on the Bladen-Loftus marriage is unimpeachable, being Lady Irwin/Loftus herself, the step-mother to Letitia Loftus and the details come from a legal case which was brought after the death of Letitia's father Dudley Loftus. Dudley's widow brought action against Letitia and Charles Bladen over her deceased husband's estate. Although the Will of Dudley Loftus has not survived[1], the case (Bunbury v Bladen) gives all the relevant information and describes the twists and turns of the Loftus family's life after Dudley's death. The (last) wife of Dr Dudley Loftus, Elizabeth Irwin, believed herself entitled to some of his estate after his death. She remarried (more than once) after Dudley Loftus died and, at the time of her taking legal action against Charles and Letitia Bladen, she was married to a Walter Bunbury.

Marital History of Mrs Dudley Loftus (2nd/last wife):

	Spouse	Marriage years	
1)	Sir Gerard Irwin[2]	1686-1688	(his death)
2)	Dr Dudley Loftus	1693-1695	(his death)
3)	Robert McNeal[3]	1695-1708	(his death)
4)	William Broughton	1710-1715	(his death)
5)	Walter Bunbury 1664-1749[4]	1720-1749	(his death)

Elizabeth lived on to 1753

Elizabeth's first husband, Sir Gerald Irwin, had died around 1689 and, after his death, she made a claim for part of his estate.[5]

---

[1] National Archives in Ireland have a note that a Will was drawn up (as for Charles Bladen) but there is scant detail as the actual Will no longer exists

[2] Oxford DNB states her name to be Lady Catherine Mervyn and that they married on 16th April 1693. This information was probably extracted from George Stokes (1900) *Some Worthies of the Irish Church* (London: Hodder). The Parish Register, however, of St John the Evangelist of Dublin states on p236 of the Representative Church Body Library edition, edited by James Mills that: Mr Dudly Loftus, Doctor of ye Law & ye Lady Elizabeth Ervin, marr'd May 11, 1693

[3] Burial of Robert Mackneale out of Queen's Bench, 26 July 1708 at St George the Martyr Church in Surrey (parish register)

[4] Marriage Settlement between Walter Bunbury of Dublin and Dame Elizabeth Irwin (aka Broughton), dated 28th/29th December 1719 (Dublin Deeds 30 388 18923), witnessed by Major Nicholas Bunbury, a Major in Sankey's Regiment which was later the 39th Dorsets. Courtesy of Peter R Bunbury and Turtle Bunbury. Also, see marriage license bond dated 1720 in Dublin

[5] Dublin Deeds: 33, 18, 19491 dated 31st October 1721, Elizabeth obtained a

By the time she married to Bunbury the frequently widowed Elizabeth had amassed a sizeable estate of her own which, before marriage, she took pains to make over to a trustee called James Kennedy.[1] She had originally brought a case over the Loftus estate in 1716 but in 1721 a new appeal was begun. In the months before the following chancery case took place (on 17 July 1721), there was a complaint brought in the House of Lords which may be relating to the same Walter Bunbury (Elizabeth's 5th husband).

"Complaint that Walter Bunbury, a menial servant of the Earl of Clarendon was arrested and imprisoned in Ireland at the suit of one Adams who, as also the attorney had used expressions derogatory to the honour and privileges of the Peers of Great Britain ...."[2]

The detail of the step-mother's case against the Bladens is produced in full below as it contains important information that provides context.[3]

Bunbury v Bolton - Cases in Parliament

Walter Bunbury Esq. And	) Appellants Case 57
Dame Elizabeth Irwin, his wife	)

Thomas Bolton, Alderman of	) Respondents
Dublin, the Reverend Dr John Bolton,	)
Dean of Derry and Charles Bladen and	)
Lettice Bladen, his wife.	)

29th November 1721
Dudley Loftus, Esq., Doctor of Laws in the year 1671, being seised in fee of several houses on the Blind Key, and in Smock Alley and Scarlet Lane, in the city of

---

Judgment against Sir Robert Adair in 1718 (under her then married/widowed name of Broughton) for part of Irwin's estate. Courtesy of Peter R Bunbury and Turtle Bunbury

[1] Dublin Deeds: 83 23 57387 dated 18th May 1734, courtesy of Peter R Bunbury and Turtle Bunbury

[2] Journal of the House of Lords 1660-1724. Edward Hyde (3rd Earl of Clarendon 1661-1724) was a colleague of Martin Bladen's, being appointed Envoy Extraordinary to Hanover in 1714

[3] Great Britain: House of Lords. Reports of Cases upon Appeals and Writs of Error in the High Court of Parliament from the year 1701 to the year 1779, Vol. 2, Dublin, p361

Dublin, mortgaged the same to the governors of the Blue-Coat Hospital near Dublin for 800 *l.* and interest at 10 per cent per ann. And a great arrear of interest being due in the year 1694, the mortgagees recovered possession of all the said mortgaged premises, except a house, which the Doctor then lived in.

On the 5th April 1695, Dr Loftus made his Will, and thereby bequeathed, inter alia, to his wife, the now appellant Lady Irwin[1], in case she survived him, the brick house within he then dwelt, with the court, garden and stable thereunto adjoining; as also all the furniture of the said house, together with one third part of the profits of all the other houses; reserving out of the said brick house, so devised as aforesaid, a room to each of his two daughters, Jane and Lettice, as, at the time of his death, should be furnished, with closets to each of them belonging. He also bequeathed to his said wife, and the respondent, Dean Bolton, the other two thirds of his real and personal estate; in trust for the said Jane and Lettice, their heirs, executors and administrators. And, if his said wife should marry after his death, then, from and after such marriage, he directed that the whole entire trust of the two thirds of his real and personal estate, should remain to Dr Bolton, as if his wife were naturally dead. And appointed the appellant, his said wife and the respondent Dean Bolton, executors of his will, and soon after died, and the executors proved the same. The appellant Lady Irwin, continued in the possession of the said brick house for some time, under the testator's Will, and possessed herself of most part of his personal estate, which she disposed of to her own use; and on the 14th of April 1695, she intermarried with one Robert McNeal.

By indenture of lease, dated the 20th of January 1696, the said Robert McNeal, and the appellant Lady Irwin, demised the said house, garden and stables &c to Thomas Milburn for the term of 21 years, if Dame Elizabeth should so long live, at the yearly rent of 55 *l.* and Milburne, by virtue of this lease, entered upon the premises, and turned the said house into a tavern, which was afterwards known by the name of the One Tun Tavern; by which means, the testator's said daughters were obliged to quit their rooms and closets, which were devised to them in the said house for their habitations. And the said McNeal, in right of his wife, received the said rent of 55 *l.* per annum from Milburne, until the year 1702, although during all that time the house was subject to the aforesaid mortgage.

In the same year 1696 some differences arising between the testator's said daughters and the appellant Lady Irwin and her husband McNeal concerning their several interests in the said mortgaged premises, they agreed to refer the same to Mr John Smith and Mr Samuel Martin, who soon made and published their award, whereby they ordered the daughters to pay 300 *l.* to the appellant Lady Irwin, in full of her interest in the said mortgaged premises, who, and also the said Robert

---

[1] Elizabeth was already known by the name Dame Elizabeth Irwin when she married Dr Loftus in 1693 (but he is not on Dr Shaw's List). She is also referred to as "relict of Sir Gerrard. Her petition shows that her husband commanded the Inniskilling forces in the late war in Ireland and died there to the petitioner's utter ruin. She is a stranger to Ireland ...." from the CSP, Domestic Series, of the Reign of Anne, 1703-4. Notes & Queries Vol. 122, William White 1910: "Lettice, only surviving child of Dudley Loftus L.LD and Frances (daughter of Patrick Nangle) married Charles Bladen"

McNeal, her then husband, knowing that after payment of the mortgage-money due to the Governors of the Blue-Coat Hospital, their demands would be of little value, were so well satisfied with this award, that in their answer to a bill filed against them by the daughters, in the year 1698, they insisted on the award, and prayed, that all the benefit and advantage thereby accruing to them might be reserved.

The mortgagees finding, that such part of the premises as they had first possessed themselves of, was not sufficient to discharge the growing interest, and much less the arrear of interest due on the mortgage; in the year 1702 brought an ejectment for recovery of the said brick houses and premises, which were let to Milburne; and having obtained judgment in such ejectment, they were afterwards put into possession of the said house. The appellant Lady Irwin and the said testator's daughters, finding that they could get nothing out of the said premises, until the principal interest and costs, due on the mortgage were fully satisfied, proposed to sell the premises to the Governors of the said Hospital, and several others, for 2000 *l.*, in which sum the principal, interest and costs due on the mortgage were to be included, but no person appearing willing to buy the same, as the buildings thereon were very old and of little value; the appellant Lady Irwin and her said husband McNeal went into England, without making any agreement about the said premises. But in the year 1704 the respondent Alderman Bolton came to an agreement with the daughters, to give 2100 *l.* for the said mortgaged premises to be paid in manner following; viz to the Governors of the Hospital 900 *l.* which then appeared to be due to them, on account of the said mortgage; 900 *l.* to the respondent Dean Bolton, in trust for the said daughters, and 300 *l.* to remain in the respondent Alderman Bolton's hands, to satisfy the appellant Lady Irwin her demands; being what she and her husband had claimed for her interest in the said premises, and what was adjudged to be the value thereof; in regard she had only an estate for life after the mortgage was discharged.

In pursuance of this agreement the said daughters and the respondent Dean Bolton, as their trustee, by deeds of lease and release, bearing date the 26th and 27th of January 1704, in consideration of 900 *l.* paid to the said respondent Dean Bolton, for the use of the said daughters, and of 12000 *l.* to be paid and retained as aforesaid, did convey and assure until the respondent Alderman Bolton and his heirs, all their estate, right and title, in and to the said premises.

In May 1706 the respondent Alderman Bolton, came to an account with the Governors of the Hospital, and there then appeared to be due on the mortgage, for principal, interest and costs 805*l.*-15s-2d and no more; they having, since the Alderman's purchase, received several sums of money out of the said premises; whereupon the said Governors, by deeds of lease and release, dated the 9th and 10th of May 1706, in consideration of 805*l.*-15s.-2d paid to them by the respondent Alderman Bolton, did assign the aforesaid mortgage to one Richard Weldon, in trust for the respondent Alderman Bolton. And by virtue of this assignment, the Alderman became possessed of all the said mortgaged premises, which, as they were then set, yielded about 120*l.* per ann.

The premises were at this time in a very ruinous condition and the expenses which the respondents, Alderman Bolton was constantly at in repairing the same, amounted to very considerable sum, so that the yearly income thereof did not answer the interest of his purchase money; and finding that no tenant would improve on the premises, and that unless the same were rebuilt, they would in a very few years, be of little or no value, he therefore let part of the said premises, to several tenants for long terms of years, who were obliged to rebuild the same houses; and who accordingly laid out great sums of money in such rebuilding, and made use of the old materials in the new buildings, so that the yearly rent of the premises, by the improvements made thereon, was increased to 1661 per ann.

The appellant Lady Irwin, being fully acquainted with all these proceedings of the respondent Alderman Bolton, seemed very well satisfied therewith, and proposed referring her demand out of the premises, to the arbitration of the respondent Dean Bolton, or any other disinterested person; but she not returning into Ireland till June 1710, and then perceiving that by the Alderman's management, the premises were in a flourishing condition, and of much greater value than when he first purchased the same; she, and her then husband William Broughton Esq on the 11th November 1710, exhibited their bill in the Court of Chancery in Ireland, against the respondents and others, praying to have the possession of the houses, which were built on the house and gardens particularly devised to her, and an account of the profits thereof, and also to have the possession of one third part of the houses built on the rest of the estate.

Pending this suit, the said William Broughton died, whereupon Dame Elizabeth on the 29th of September 1715, obtained an order to proceed in the cause in her own name. Accordingly, on the 21st of November 1716, the cause was heard before the Lord Chancellor; when his Lordship was pleased to order and decree, inter alia, that the appellant Lady Irwin should recover from the respondent, Alderman Bolton, the house called the One Tun, with the garden, stables and appurtenances thereto belonging; and that so much of the premises as were let to Milburne, should be accounted for at 55 *l.* per ann. During Milburn's lease; and after the expiration thereof, that the appellant should have, during her natural life, the rents of the said demised premises then let by the respondent Alderman Bolton; and a third part of the rest of the real estate during her natural life, as the same was then let by the respondent Alderman Bolton, subject to a fifth part of the mortgage assigned by the Blue Coat Hospital, to the respondent Alderman Bolton. And that the fines received by him from the tenants, should go towards discharge of the incumbrances.

The respondent, the Alderman, apprehending himself aggrieved by some part of this decree, intended to apply for a rehearing of the cause, but was prevented by Lady Irwin's inrolling the decree; he therefore submitted, and in the course of about five years, he paid Lady Irwin upwards of 500 *l.* in part performance of it.

But, after this acquiescence, and after Lady Irwin had married Mr Bunbury, they thought proper to appeal from this decree; because it directed that the house, and so much of the premises as were let to Milburne, should be accounted for, during his lease at 55 *l.* per ann; whereas he paid 55 *l.* per ann for one part of what was let to him, and 5 *l.* per ann for other part thereof, as appeared by the proofs in the cause; and therefore what was so let to him ought to be accounted for, during the time of his lease at 60 *l.* per ann. That after Milburne's lease, the appellant Dame Elizabeth was decreed to have, during her life, only the rent of the premises, as let by the respondent Alderman Bolton, whereas he purchasing the reversion from the two daughters, and afterwards taking in the mortgage, with full notice of the appellant Dame Elizabeth's estate for life, and so becoming voluntarily concerned; he ought not to put her in a worse condition than she would have been, had he not been so concerned: and therefore the appellant Dame Elizabeth ought not to be concluded for her life interest, at an under rent reserved on fines taken by the Alderman; but ought to have possession of the house and garden particularly devised to her, with all the improvements thereon, or an equivalent for the same, according to the improved rents thereof, and likewise for the materials of the old houses. That as to the third part of the rest of the estate, devised to the appellant Dame Elizabeth, she was decreed only to the third part of the rents at present received, tho' great fines had been taken on making the leases and the reversion thereby unduly eased and improved at her charge. That these fines which were chiefly taken out of her estate for life, were decreed to be applied in satisfaction of the mortgage and no recompense was decreed to her, though she ought only to bear a proportion of that mortgage; so that the appellants were unequally charged, in ease of the reversion, for when the mortgage was paid, Dame Elizabeth was, during the remainder of her life, to have only the rents reserved, where such fines had been taken. That there was no direction given by the decree, that the appellant Dame Elizabeth should have interest coming to her from the respondent Alderman Bolton, whilst the same lay in his hands, nor was the consideration of interest reserved; neither were the respondents decreed to produce before the Mater upon oath, all deeds, writings and accounts, in their custody or power; which ought to have been done and without which the account could not be fairly taken and adjusted. That the respondents ought also to have been decreed to be examined on interrogatories to discover what was bona fide paid on the mortgage, and likewise for clearing the accounts and other matters in question, as there should be occasion; and the rather, because the mortgagees were in receipt of the rents and profits of the premises, for about ten years before the assignment to respondent Alderman Bolton, whereby the mortgage was very near, if not fully satisfied; and the appellant Dame Elizabeth, ought to have been decreed her costs. That the personal estate of Dr Loftus ought to have been in the first place applied towards satisfaction of the mortgage; and what the appellant Dame Elizabeth had paid towards the discharge thereof, ought to be reimbursed her out of such personal estate, or out of the two thirds belonging to the coheirs. And therefore it was hoped that in these several particulars, the decree would be altered and amended.

To this it was answered, on the other side, that it did not appear by any proof in the cause, that Milburne paid 55 *l.* per ann. For one part, and 5 *l.* for another; but it manifestly appeared by the lease, that he only paid 55 *l.* per ann. That it was apprehended, the appellant Lady Irwin could have no more than the rent of the house, during Milburne's lease; and if the respondent Alderman Bolton, who was assignee of the mortgage, had not managed in the manner before mentioned, in letting all the mortgaged premises to improving tenants for long terms of years, the same would not have yielded more than the interest of the mortgage, and then Lady Irwin could not thereout have received anything. That the Alderman took no fines out of the premises demised to Milburne, but what fines he did take, were out of the rest of the real estate, in which Lady Irwin was only interested as to one third; and therefore her interest could in no respect be thereby lessened, in regard she was to pay one fifth part of the mortgage, and consequently could only be entitled to one fifth part of the fines. That it was not insisted, at the hearing of the cause, that the respondent Alderman Bolton should pay Lady Irwin interest, nor did the court see any reason for directing interest; that Alderman being always ready to pay, what in justice Lady Irwin was entitled to and did, in fact, advance, and pay her several sums of money, before any became due. That all the deeds, writings and accounts were proved in the cause, and therefore of course must be produced before the Master; and if there had been any such defect in the decree, as is now pretended, the Court would have rectified it upon a motion. And, as to the examining Alderman Bolton upon personal interrogatories, it was not insisted upon at the hearing; but if the Court had seen any reason for it, this also might have been supplied by a motion. Besides, it was proved in the cause, that the Alderman paid 805*l.*-15s-2d to the governors of the Hospital, which appeared to be then due to them on the mortgage; and that the account was approved of by the daughters, and by the respondent the Dean as their trustee. And as to the costs, considering how fair the respondent had abated, it was not reasonable that costs should be decreed against them; and the rather, because the respondent Alderman Bolton stood in the place of a mortgagee, as well as a purchaser of the reversion, and since the appellant Lady Irwin had inrolled the decree, acquiesced under it for five years, and received upwards of 500*l.* by virtue thereof; and would not, under her uncertain estate for life, have ever reaped any benefit from the premises in question, without the methods taken by the Alderman for the improvements of them, it was hoped that the decree would be affirmed, and appeal dismissed with costs.

ACCORDINGLY, after hearing counsel on this appeal, it was ORDERED and ADJUDGED that the same should be dismissed; and the decree therein complained of, affirmed: and it was further ORDERED, that the appellants should pay to the respondents the sum of 40*l.* for their costs, in respect of the said appeal.

Bolton and the Bladens, therefore, successfully counteracted the Bunbury suit and Walter and Elizabeth Bunbury (née Irwin) were required to compensate the Bladens their costs. It seems likely that this was the same Walter Bunbury who had a contract dispute with Dr Thomas Bladen in May of 1690, in which case the two families had a long history of feuding. His new wife Elizabeth, having Letitia Bladen (née Loftus) as a step-daughter, may have resurrected Bunbury's animosity towards Charles Bladen, in lieu of the deceased father Dr Thomas. Walter Bunbury went on to serve as an MP for Bannow in County Wexford and Clonmines. He was also active in government, serving on numerous committees.

One hundred years later, in 1820, there was a further dispute which was connected to the above mentioned estate of Dudley Loftus. It concerned who had the power to control the advowson of Ratoath

Church in County Meath and which necessitated the close examination of historical records. It was said that Dudley Loftus acquired the advowson from his father and, in the course of the dispute, depositions were made which effectively mapped out the history of the contentious advowson and which shows how it came through Bladen hands:-

Advowson of Ratoath Church (Meath):
To: 1622 - The Crown
    1622 - Sir William Parsons
    1628 - Adam Loftus - Presented Henry Bolton to vicarage
    1663 - Dudley Loftus (acquired from father)-Presented Noah Webb 1675, John Bolton 1677
    1695 - Charles Bladen=Letitia Loftus (acquired from father), trustee John Bolton also had right
        of Presentation
    1708 - Trustee John Bolton purchased advowson in 1708 from the Bladens for £10
    1720 - Rev. John Bolton resigned, Crown presented Richard Bolton: Rev Bolton's sons: Thomas
        Richard and Joseph
    1761 - Thomas Bolton presented Rev Thomas Norman
    1793 - Rev Thomas Norman devised to trustees (Gardiner/Blessington et al)
    1794 - Crown's turn to present Rev L K Conyngham
    1820 - Lord Blessington, as heir-at-law to surviving trustee claimed his right to present[1]

One of the parties who declared a right to the advowson was a Mrs Fox who claimed she was a descendant of Dudley Loftus, through Letitia (Mrs Bladen). Sadly, however, Mrs Fox lost her case as she was unable to prove her descent to the court's satisfaction and Lord Blessington succeeded to the advowson.

---

[1] The Ecclesiastical Register containing the names of the dignitaries and parochial clergy of Ireland, as also of the parishes and their respective patrons, and an account of monies granted for building churches and glebe houses with ecclesiastical annals, 1827

10. OTHER BLADENS

Sarah Bladen (née Blayney)

The last wife of Dr Thomas Bladen was Sarah Blayney c1630-1722 who appears not to have had any children. She managed to outlive him by 25 years and her Will, which can be seen on page 91, gives an insight into her life and relations. Her family gave the name to Castleblayney, about 60 miles from Dublin, which is located next to Lake Muckno in County Monaghan. During the Rebellion of 1641-42 the whole family, including Sarah, were imprisoned for some time when Castleblayney was seized and her father Lord Henry was slain by rebels in 1646 at the Battle of Benburgh in County Tyrone.

Sarah owned/inherited property in the Manor of Muckno for which she received a rental income and she bequested that, together with most of her other possessions, to her Coningsby cousins.[1] Sarah had an impressive ancestry, not just because her father was Lord Henry Blayney but her grandmother was Anne Loftus, daughter of the Protestant Archbishop Adam Loftus.[2] One of her Loftus cousins had married into the Coningsby family and the Earl and his relations became Sarah's main beneficiaries in her Will.[3]

At the time she wrote her Will Sarah was residing at one of the Coningsby family's homes in Albemarle Street in London, her Will left bequests to the Earl's chaplain and servants in London.

---

[1] Lady Frances Jones (daughter of Richard, 1st Earl of Ranelagh) had been disinherited by her father when she married Thomas 1st Earl of Coningsby. Her two daughters then became Sarah Bladen's principal beneficiaries, along with their widowed father

[2] Archbishop Adam Loftus 1533-1605, Lord Chancellor of Ireland

[3] Thomas, 1st Earl of Coningsby was the grandfather of Hon. Frances Hanbury-Williams who married William Capel, 4th Earl of Essex, as his first wife. Capel's second wife was Harriet Bladen, grand-daughter of William Bladen from the Yorkshire branch of the family (William became Attorney-General in Maryland). It was through the Earl of Coningsby that Hampton Court, the 15th Century Castle - not to be confused with Hampton Court Palace royal residence, descended to Harriet Bladen's husband's former father-in-law Sir Charles Hanbury-Williams who sold it to Richard Arkwright of Cromford in Derbyshire. The Art Journal, Vol. 33, 1871

The Earl of Coningsby, who was mentioned several times in the Will, held numerous posts in the government and Sarah Bladen made his daughters her executors and heirs to her estate in Ireland.

William Bladen

Alderman William Bladen's younger son William (c1616->69) was probably born in London, like his elder brother and at the age of 10 years he travelled with his family to Dublin. He was also in the print trade, probably apprenticed to his father as he later stated he had always lived with his father in Dublin, and was freed of his 7 year apprenticeship at the age of 25 in 1641 according to records of the Stationers Company.

William was heavily involved in his father's printing and bookselling business but he was not present in Ireland in 1641 during the Irish Rebellion, he was in fact in London at the time running the Bladen family's book-selling and printing business there. When the House of Lords petitioned his father to send accurate reports of the situation following the rebellion in Ireland,[1] William stated that he had "always lived with his father, an Alderman of Dublin" and that both he and his father were "well acquainted with the affairs of Ireland". He produced and distributed some 10 pamphlets from the information his father sent to him.

In 1642, like his older brother Thomas, William advanced money to Cromwell for the use of the parliamentary forces as an Adventurer, seeking the opportunity to be recompensed with land in Ireland afterwards.[2]

William oversaw the Bladen family's print interest in London during the early 1640s where he traded as a bookseller at Fleet Street, London in 1641. His father's letters from Ireland were directed to William and he was requested to have them printed and brought to the public's attention, which he did. In 1647 William was on a visit to Dublin where he witnessed his father's appointment as Mayor.

The last we hear of William was in 1669 where he presented his father's apprentice Nathaniel Thompson to the Stationers Company.

---

[1] HMC, 4th Report, p113b

[2] CSP state: 1st March 1642."William Bladen stationer of Dublin (son of [Alderman]) to be paid £500 to those who have advanced money to the companies in the army"

Samuel Bladon

One last Bladon name worth mentioning in connection with the Irish Bladens is Samuel 1723-99. James Raven in his 2007 book 'The Business of Books: Booksellers and the English Book Trade 1450-1850' makes reference to the continuity of the Bladen/Bladon family in the bookselling business *'so did the Newbery and Bladon families continue in unbroken (but now obscure) lines of business from the sixteenth to the eighteenth century and beyond"*. These connections are, indeed, obscure and lost to time but it does seem likely that there is a direct connection between Alderman William Bladen and his sons and the emergence as a bookseller of Samuel Bladon at no. 28 (from 1767-1773) and later no. 13 Paternoster Row between 1778 and 1796. Samuel was involved in bookselling and newspaper publishing (he started the Daily Courant, the first newspaper) but also was responsible for producing over 800 titles as either publisher or seller. His trading locations were either at St Paul's Churchyard (where Alderman William and his family had resided and worked) or, later, at Paternoster Row.[1] Raven describes how 'Bladon's shop was oddly sandwiched between the linked shops occupied by James Rivington and then by Crowder ...'.

Samuel's Will of 1799 listed his address at death as being Andersons Buildings on City Road but did not mention any family; he may, therefore, have been unmarried as most bequests were to various cousins and fellow booksellers. His executor was Joseph Vigevena,[2] a Jewish merchant who was involved in the print trade.[3] Other relations referred to in his Will were Mowrys, children of his sister Margaret who married Anthony Mowry in 1753.

The difficulty of linking Samuel Bladon, bookseller and printer, to Alderman William and his family may stem from the possibility that Samuel and his sister may have descended from a single mother. Samuel died in 1799, aged 76 years and the choice of Bunhill Fields Cemetery for his burial may indicate that he was a non-conformist or a Quaker.

---

[1] He was also stated in a Will to be a warehouseman of Andrew Millar

[2] It is possible that Joseph was not so much a type printer than involved in copper-plate printing

[3] No doubt some relation to him was Sarah Vigevena who was listed as a stationers company apprentice at the time

As Samuel was born in 1723 he could well have been a descendant of one of Alderman William Bladen's children but there has been no evidence found to substantiate that, only the circumstantial evidence of him being in the same trade at the same location.

EPILOGUE

What must it have been like for a young 15-year-old from Newton Solney on the south bank of the River Trent in the heart of the countryside to be sent off to the centre of London? To be committed to a seven year apprenticeship in a London rife with plague in the final years of the Elizabethan era? We can only guess how he felt and, though some would have found the experience daunting, it seems that William thrived on it. Bladen spent 25 years there and, after completing his apprenticeship, branched out to run his own book-selling and print business in the capital.

Perhaps the same spirit which helped him adapt to a move to London also gave him the courage to take his family to Dublin when he was around 40 years of age. The Bladens traded of course to increase their own prosperity but they also became an integral part of the Anglo-Irish Protestant community and William took an active part in the Dublin administration. To his credit, he remained in the city when many of his wealthy English friends fled in fear when the Rebellion began in 1641 and, if the Bladens' fortunes waxed and waned during their times in Ireland, then it is hardly surprising for there could not be a more turbulent era to live through.

The shock of discovering the plan to overthrow the administration at Dublin Castle in October of that year may have led to some Protestant accounts of Rebel atrocities being exaggerated. William had been embarrassed by those stories when he heard about them and sought to write his own entirely truthful accounts. His 'journals' of the Irish Rebellion were the truth so far as he could ascertain it from first-hand accounts and, of course, they were written by someone who lived through events and, like all the other reports that were reaching England, they did contribute to a general state of alarm.

At least three generations of Bladens resided in Ireland and many descendants today with the Bladen surname are descended from this family.

Karen Proudler

APPENDICES

Will of Alderman William Bladen 1585-1663

In the Name of God, Amen, yet twenty-sixth day of April one thousand six hundred and sixtie-two (1662) I William Bladen of the parish of Saint Warburs [St Werburgh's] in the citie of Dublin, Alderman, being weak in bodie but of sound and perfect memorie, praise be given to God for the same and knowing the uncertaintie of this life in earth and being desirous to settle things in order doe make this my Last Will and Testament in manner and form following. First and principally I recommend my soule to Almightie God my creator assuredly believing I shall receive full pardon and true remission of all my sins and be saved by the precious death and merits of my blessed Saviour and Redeemer Christ Jesus. And my bodie to the earth from whence it was taken to be buried in such descent and Christian manner as to my Executrix hereafter named shall be thought moote and convenient. And as touching such worldly estate as the Lord in mercy hath lent me, my Will and meaning is the same shall be imployed and bestowed as hereafter by this my Will is expressed. And first I do revoke renounce and make voyd all Wills and Deeds of Gifts by me formerly made and declare and appoint this my Last Will and Testament. Item I do give and bequeath unto my dearlie beloved wife Ellinor Bladen all my money, plate, jewels, brass, pewter, linen and all other my household goods whatever. Item I give and bequeath unto my said wife the lease of our house in Sheep Street, Dublin and of our piece of ground near Saint Stephen's Green Dublin called Flints Park and one other piece of ground near the 'Hogg and Butts' in the occupation of John Sammes all which I had in marriage with her. The premises to be in her dispose as she shall think fit. Item my will and meaning that all my stock in the shop, printing house and the warehouses, both in Dublin and London together with the interest I have in my now dwelling house and printing house and the house next door to my said dwelling house now in the occupation of Master Keating shall be sold unto some person or persons having served seven years to a print stationer or bookseller and the money arising thereby my debts and funeral expenses first satisfied, the rest to be disposed of as follows (viz: one third part thereof I give unto my said wife, one other part third part to my sonne Doctor Thomas Bladen and the other third part unto my said sonne's children to be equally distributed betwixt them yet notwithstanding my will and meaning is that in the disposal of my aforesaid dwellinghouse my said wife shall have use occupy, possess and enjoy the two chambers next the street with the little room over the first stairs wherein my wife's daughter lodges with free carriage and way thereto as shall be fitting during her widowhood. Item I give and bequeath unto my kinsman Jeremiah Rotherham of Birmingham in the countie of Stafford in England twenty pounds. To my servant John Loath, conditionally to be careful to get in my debts ten pounds. To Mary Lynager my maidservant three pounds. To Master Sam Cox, the minister five pounds. To the churchwarden of the parish of St Werburghs towards the putting forth poor children ten pounds. To the said churchwardens to be disposed of to six poor widows of the said parish whom they judge to stand most in need thereof at fortie shillings each. Twelve pounds to Joane Mason widow. Fortie shillings to my overseers hereafter named at five pounds. Twenty five pounds to Elizabeth Johnson, twenty shillings. To Margaret Pemberton, my wife's mother in law. Four pounds to James Rimner of Upton. Fortie shillings to my maidservant Anne Bennett. Twenty shillings to my sister Anne her two daughters, eight shillings each. All which legacies aforementioned amounting to one hundred pounds. My will is shall be paid to the respective persons within three months after my decease by my executor hereafter named and lastly I do appoint my said wife Ellinor Bladen sole executor and Thomas Richardsons, Nathaniel Boys, Esq., William Phillips, Captain Enoch Riden and Lieutenant Thomas Wright overseers of this my last will and testament. In witness whereof I have hereunto put my name and affixed my seal the day and year first above written. Memorandum, my will and meaning is that if any of my widow's third part shall be unpaid at the time of her death, shall be paid to my son Thomas Bladen aforesaid and his children. William Bladen signed and sealed in the witness of those whose name as subscribed after the addition of the two last lines and underlining the words (any of). William Collis, John Loath and Thomas Wright. Probatum London - Anglicana[1].

---

[1] TNA: PROB 11/313 Will of Alderman William Bladen

Will of Eleanor Bladen - Alderman William's wife

In the Name of God Amen,[1] the twentieth day of March in the twentieth year of the raigne of our Sovereign Lord King Charles the Second [Anno] in one thousand six hundred and sixty seven (1667) I Eleanor Bladen of the city of Dublin, widow, being sick and weak of body but of sound and perfect memory, praise be given to God for the same and knowing the uncertainty of this life on earth and being desirous to settle things in order, doe make and ordain this to be my last will and testament in manner and form following. That is to say, first and principally I commend my soul to Almighty God, my creator, assuredly believing that I shall receive full pardon and true remission of all my sins and be saved by the precious death and merits of my blessed Saviour and Redeemer Christ Jesus and my body to the earth from whence it was taken to be buried in such decent manner as my executors hereafter named shall think fit under the gravestone of my late husband, Mr Thomas Pemberton in the churchyard of St Werburgh's church within the city of Dublin. And my desire is that Mr Rigby, Minister of St Katherine's parish within the suburbs of the city of Dublin will be pleased to preach my funeral sermon and, for his pains therein I give and bequeath unto him the sum of £5 sterling and as for such worldly goods which the Lord had blessed me with I give and bequeath as follows. Item I give and bequeath to my loving kinswoman Mrs Jane Jones the sum of £20 sterling current and lawful money of England. Item, I give and bequeath unto my servant Margery Buxton £20 sterling of current and lawful money of England. Item I give unto my loving friend Mrs Purefoy the sum of £20 of good and lawful money of England. Item I give and bequeath unto my kinswoman Elizabeth Woods ten pounds sterling of current and lawful money. Item, I give unto Margaret Birstall five pounds sterling of good and lawful money. Item, I give and bequeath unto my kinsman Robert Armstrong £5 sterling current and lawful money of England. And my will and meaning is that the several legacies by me bequeathed as aforesaid shall be paid out of that one hundred pounds sterling which I lately put into the hands of Richard Young of Dublin, solicitor, towards purchasing of a house for me in Castle Yard Street (or Grafton Yard Street) Dublin and by seisin under his hand and seal appeared. Now I give and bequeath unto my said kinswoman Margery Burton my two gold rings which I usually wear on the thumb of my left hand. Now I give and bequeath unto Elizabeth Woods 40 shillings sterling to buy her a gold ring. Item I give and bequeath unto my kinsman John Roe and my kinswoman Eleanor Roe, son and daughter of my brother Peter Roe in England that £40 sterling which their said father gave unto me to be equally divided betwixt them when their said father shall pay the same. And my will and meaning is that the several legacies by me bequeathed as aforesaid shall be paid by my executors hereafter named within three months after my demise. Item my will and meaning is, and I do hereby give and bequeath all the rest of my goods and chattels, gold rings, plate, silver and woollen, my debts and legacies being paid, unto my dearly beloved daughter Anne Pemberton and my will and desire is that my said daughter may continue with my said kinswoman Mrs Jane Jones and my said kinswoman Margaret Burton or with either of them as my said daughter shall think fit during her life. And further my will and meaning is that whenceforth my said daughter shall happen to depart this life, that then all my goods and chattels shall be given and equally divided betwixt my said kinsman John Roe and my kinswoman Eleanor Roe within six months next after my said daughter's demise and my will and meaning is that my said kinswoman Jane Jones and Margery Burton be paid by my executors hereafter named for my said daughter's dyett, clothes and attendance by a mayde servant such and so much money quarterly and every quarter of a year during the life of my said daughter, shall continue with either of them or they, or either of them, shall demand and think fit. And lastly I nominate and ordaine my loving friend Richard Young of Dublin, solicitor, and John North of the same, stationer, my full and whole executors of this my last will and testament to this my will p'formed and my estate p'formed for my said daughter and for their care and pains therein I give and bequeath unto the said Richard Young £10 sterling and likewise I give and bequeath unto the said John North and Maudlin, his wife, all my stock of goods and money whatsoever which I have, or of right out to have, within the city of London and suburbs thereof.

In witness whereof I have hereunto put my hand and seale and published this to be my last will and testament, the day and year first about written. John Mayor, Mary Plumm £5 sterlin E.B. of Eleanor Bladen. Signed sealed and published and signed with the mark of William Griffin, B.G. Thomas, Mr Clarrish, Edward B. Wood

---

[1] TNA: PROB 11/327 Will of Eleanor Bladen

Will of Sarah Bladen (née Blayney)

I Sarah Bladen[1] of Albemarle Street in the parish of St Martin do make this my Last Will and Testament in manner and form following revoking all former Wills. I do bequeath my soul unto God, my body to be buried in whatever parish I die. My funeral to be very private and with as little expense as it can be made. I give and bequeath to the Lady Dwr Countess Coningsby and Lady Frances Coningsby daughter of the Rt Hon the Earl Coningsby by his late wife Lady Frances Coningsby and to their heirs and assigns for ever all that my yearly rent charge of £50 a year due to me and payable unto my heirs or assigns out of the Lordship or Manor of Mucknow in the County of Monaghan in the Kingdom of Ireland. I do nominate, constitute and appoint the Lady Countess Coningsby and the Lady Frances Coningsby my executors of this my Last Will and Testament as witness my hand and seal this 3rd day of October One Thousand Seven Hundred and Twenty. S. Bladen. Witnesses present at the signing and sealing; Mary Ladybird, Butler Lacy and Thomas Dawes. My funeral to be as private and as little expenses as is possible to be made, my body to be laid in the parish church in whatever parish I die, the expense not to exceed 15 pounds. Two rings to be given, as I have set them down 25 shillings apiece the rings, rings to be given: Earl Coningsby, Lady Coningsby, Lady Frances Coningsby, Lady Thanet, Lady Kildare, Lady Catherine Jones, my cousin Moore*, Mr Partenton, Earl Coningsby's Chaplain, Lady Wentworth, to Earl Coningsby's London servants ten shillings a piece to buy gloves which will be about 8 pounds, to Ann Butts to buy mourning, to Ann Butts, if she be with me when I die my cabinet screen, all my wearing clothes, both linen and woollen and all that belongs to my person, my china, and all my sheets towels and napkins and also a featherbed, bolster and blankets and bedstead and tables and what belongs to my bedroom. As witness my hand this fourth of October 1720. S. Bladen, B Lacy, T Dawes. There is to defray the charges of my funeral and my maid remains in my Lord Coningsby's hand £68-19-0d. In money in the green purse £44-11s-0d which is now put into the African October the 11th 42 guineas and eleven shillings. Silver is put into the African Company, October 11th, 1720.

William Bladen, 1592

"In the Name of God Amen, the xxii day of June anno domini 1592, I Wylliam Bladon of Newton Soilne in the county of Derby do make my testament and last wyll in manor and form as followeth. First I bequeath my soulle to Almyghtie God the father the sonne and the hollye ghost bye whose meritorious death and blood-shedding I trust only to be saved and by none other means. And my body to the earth where it shall please God to call me. Item I give and bequeath to every one of my children's children xii d. Item I give to Thomas Hill my son-in-law one dozen ewes. Item I give to every one of my god-children lyving xiv. Item I give to the Pynfold Brydge xij. Item I give to the Dale Brydge xid. Item I give to William Bladen my sheppard one ewe lamb. Item I give to William Green and Margaret Eveherd my servants to either of them one ewe lamb. Item I give to Agnes Newton the daughter of Nicholas Newton my son-in-law one heffer calf of a year old. Item I give to the children of Richard Hyndgler of Twyford xxi and then one further calf of a year only to be delivered to them one whole year after that the first is delivered and no more, until my wyll and until my funeral expenses is discharged and all my debts payde, then Thomas my son, whom I make and appoynt to be my executor shall have and injoy all the rest of my goods and cattells and chattels moveable and immovable, whatsoever, also I make overseers hereof Rychard Hingdley and Nicholas Newton."

---

[1] TNA: PROB 11/584, Will of Sarah Bladen (née Blayney, wife of Dr Thomas Bladen)

CHRONOLOGIES

Alderman William Bladen

1585	Born at Newton Solney, son of Thomas (yeoman), baptised Egginton, Derbyshire on 23rd February 1585
1602	1st May: Printers Apprenticeship with Arthur Johnson, St Paul's Churchyard, London
1604	Brother Richard was also a Printers Apprenticeship in London with Humphrey Hooper
1610	7th May: Obtained his Freedom of the Stationers Company
1610-26	Traded as a book-seller/printer at St Paul's Churchyard in London, Bay H, the Latin Shop
1612	13th Apr: Married Mary Yonge at St Bride's, Fleet Street, London
1612-31	Obtained various loans from the Stationers Company to fund his business start up
1612	In partnership in the book trade with John Royston
1612-24	Traded at St Paul's Cathedral Churchyard at the sign of the Bible by the great north door
1612-24	Rented a house at the same place for £15 in Bay H (the Latin Shop at St Paul's)
c1615	Birth of eldest son Thomas
c1616	Birth of younger son William
1618-19	Visiting Ireland on occasions
1626	Prepared to leave London for Ireland (sold copies to Edward Brewster)
1626	August: To Dublin, Ireland where he joined up with Arthur Johnson former Master
1631	Freed by the City of Dublin by special grace and favour (£10 fine)
1631	Arthur Johnson died and, as his assistant, William took over
1631	Bought the Irish Stock and became Dublin Factor
1634	Bought stock of books from Chester
1634	John Bladen (Yorkshire) visits Radcliffe/Wentworth Dublin Castle
1637	Summer: sent his servant James Redway to New England to buy land/house for him
1637-38	Elected Sheriff of Dublin
1639	2nd September: Admitted to the livery of the Stationers Company
1639	Bought stock of books from Chester
1639	Dissolution of partnership with Stationers Company
1639	Agreed to buy out the Irish stock for £2,600 (only paid £974-5s-8d in total)
1639	Acquired the Patent as the King's Printer in Ireland
1639	Elected Alderman of Dublin (other records state this was 1642)
1641	Bought stock of books from Chester
1641-42	Under siege in Dublin Castle during the Irish Rebellion

1642	Jan-May: Sent reports of the Rebellion to son William in London to publish
1642	1st March: Paid £500 - as one who had advanced money to the Army
1642-47	King's Printer
1643	Lived in Castle Street, Dublin
1647	September: Elected Mayor of Dublin
1654	Married Eleanor Pemberton
1659	Lived in St Werburgh's Street, a very short distance from Castle Street
1660	Lost the title of King's Printer to John Crooke of London
1662	26th April: Wrote his Will
1662	29th April: Petitioned the Lord Lieutenant of Ireland for money owed to him for State Printing
1663	July: Died

Dr Thomas Bladen

c1615	Born probably in London
1626	Went to Ireland with his family
1631-37	Attended Trinity College, Dublin
1641	Under siege with the Digby family at Geashill Castle
1645-56	25th Mar: Vicar of St Margaret's Church, Rainham, Kent
1653	Lent money to Cromwell's Adventurers
1654	20th Jan: Power from Thomas to cousin William Leggett to draw his lot for a barony in Armagh
1654	23rd Feb: Drew his lot for various baronies in Armagh, Down and Antrim
1654	10th Oct: Warrant to pay Thomas £50 to travel to Ireland to preach
1654	Father married Eleanor Pemberton
1654	Minister of Duleek (just north of Dublin)
1650	8th Aug: Marriage to Martha Spencer, St Peter-le-Poer, London
1655	16th May: Pass to go to Ireland: Thomas with wife, mother, child and servant (Thomas, son of Mr Bladen, merchant of Dublin)
1656	24th Jan: Petition from Thomas for £50 to go to Ireland [to preach]
1656	Left his ministry at Rainham in Kent
1656	Petition for £50 allowance for Thomas to travel to Ireland
1657	17th Mar: Marriage to Catherine Turner at St Michan's, Dublin
1658	Minister of Drogheda
1660	Prebend of Dunlavin at St Patrick's Cathedral
1662	27th June: Rector of Kilskeire (County Meath) north of Dublin
1662	September: Appointed Chaplain-in-Ordinary to the Duke of Ormond
1663	Father's death. Will left one-third of his estate to Thomas's children
1665	Bladen produces books under the imprint of Nathaniel Thompson
1666	Appointed Dean of Artfert (West Ireland)
1667	Bladen produces books for Dudley Loftus
1671	An Order of Council forbids Thomas from printing
1673	A Final Order from the Council to seize his press
1677	Dean of two daughters, both buried St John the Evangelist Church,

Dublin

1680	Thomas and family resident at 14 Fishamble Street, Dublin
1680	Took possession of Lord Roper's monument over a debt dispute
1681	Dean of St Andrew's in Dublin
1681	Bladen fails in his application to be Dean to replace Ezekiel Hopkins, Bp of Raphoe
1681	Purchased 2½ cwt of books from Chester
1690	2nd May: Dean of St Patricks complained Thomas made infrequent sermons
1690	Death of second wife
1691	28th July: Marriage to Sarah Blayney at St Martin's London (she died 28th February 1722)
1693	11th May: Officiated at the wedding of Dr Dudley Loftus and Lady Elizabeth Irwin
1695	Dean of Ardfert, Western Ireland
1695	Death, and burial on 4th July 1695
1695	Wife Sarah, resident in London with Thomas's children: Sarah, Ann and Thomas

www.ingramcontent.com/pod-product-compliance
Lightning Source LLC
Chambersburg PA
CBHW072208270326
41930CB00011B/2576